Feng Shui Demystified Revised Edition

Clear Englebert

iUniverse, Inc.
New York   Bloomington

Feng Shui Demystified Revised Edition

iUniverse books may be ordered through booksellers or by contacting:

iUniverse
1663 Liberty Drive
Bloomington, IN 47403
www.iuniverse.com
1-800-Authors (1-800-288-4677)

Because of the dynamic nature of the Internet, any Web addresses or links contained in this book may have changed since publication and may no longer be valid.

ISBN: 978-1-4401-9804-5 (sc)
ISBN: 978-1-4401-9803-8 (ebk)

First edition published in 2000 by The Crossing Press
Cover design by Rick Mears
Cover photograph by Steve Mann, of rock wall and entry designed by Christina Birtcher
Illustrations by Rick Mears and Steve Mann
Photo of Clear Englebert by James Scott Geras

Printed in the United States of America

iUniverse rev. date: 1/8/2010

Contents

Preface viii

Introduction ix

Chapter 1: The Exterior 1
    Front Door 6
    Foreboding Objects 8
    Lay of the Land 10

Chapter 2: Chi Flow 12
    Loss of Chi 13
    Clutter 15
    Empowered Positions 19
    Poison Arrows 24
    Attracting Chi 28

Chapter 3: Introduction to the Bagua 34
    Chart of Bagua Areas 38
    Elemental Cycles 40

Chapter 4: The Bagua in Place 43
    Applying the Bagua 46
    Individual Bagua Areas 49
    Bathroom Location 58

Chapter 5: Extensions and Missing Areas 62
    Bringing Back a Missing Area 64
    Windowboxes 65

Chapter 6: Architectural Features 68
    Doors 68
    Windows 71
    Poles 72
    Fireplaces 73
    Split-Level Houses 74
    Kitchens 74
    Home Offices 76
    Bedrooms 76
    Ceiling 78

Roof 78
High-rise Apartments and Condos. 79
Air Circulation 79

Chapter 7: Furniture and Household Objects 80
  Beds 80
Glass Tabletops 81
Altars. 82
Clocks 83
Mirrors 83
Symbolism. 85
Living Room Furnishings 86

Chapter 8: Other Considerations. 87
Yin/Yang 87
Lot Shape 89
Repairs and Renovations 91
Details. 93
Guests 94
Cars. 95
Other Vehicles 97
EMFs. 97
Pregnancy 98
Ashes 99
The Number Four 99
Organizing. 99
Vibrational Cleansing 100
Used Objects 102
Non-Feng Shui Techniques 102

Chapter 9: Moving 104
Locating a New Home. 104
Checklist for Moving. 106

Chapter 10: Gardening 110
Landscaping. 110
Pruning 111
The Five Elements 112
The Bagua Outside 113
Houseplants. 114
Thorny Plants 114

Chapter 11: Retail Stores. 116

The Front. 116
Physical Layout 117
Business Hours 118
Websites 119

Chapter 12:   Offices **120**
Waiting Rooms 121

Chapter 13:   Recommended Reading. **122**
Related Topics 126

Glossary **128**

Acknowledgments. **133**

Sources **134**

Index. **135**

About the Author **139**

Preface

Bigger is definitely better in the case of this new edition. It's been nine years since *Feng Shui Demystified* was first published, and this new edition is greatly revised to include more situations, more solutions, and more success stories. One of the most useful new additions is the Checklist for Moving. Note that this new edition has fewer pages than the earlier edition. That's to save paper and trees. There are lots more words, just less white space.

The more you do something, the better you get at it. I continue to practice and teach feng shui because clients report amazing results. "It was like a dam burst!" "My whole life changed!"

The two things that are still left out of this book are consumerism and superstition—no "lucky" objects or directions, just the knowledge of the energetics of *form* and *symbolism*.

Introduction

It is pronounced *fung shway* and it means wind/water. It is the part of ancient Chinese Taoism that is concerned with how objects affect energy and how that energy affects your life. It has survived four millennia because it actually works. Feng shui isn't something you have to take on faith. If done correctly, it can prove itself for anyone. Some aspects of feng shui seem like common sense, while others seem like total superstition. There are about as many different kinds of feng shui as there are kinds of Christianity.

Even though feng shui came from the East, and partakes of those philosophies, it is very much concerned with universal energetics. It is wise to education yourself as to how energy flows and to know how the things around you are influencing you. The way certain chairs are positioned can make a big difference in how prepared you are for the future. The shape of the landscape around your home *is* influencing you. The location of knives and the shape of windows can say something about how people get along with one another in a particular house.

Some aspects of Western interior design and architecture are anathema to feng shui. The following are quite common, and are considered to be serious problems:

- Walls of glass (which let chi leak out fast).
- Glass tabletops (acting like blades, cutting you off from reaching your goals).
- Open beams (which radiate poison arrows to the space below them).

Some items associated with feng shui clash with sleek modern design. Windchimes (where there is no wind), hanging flutes, big fake firecrackers, statues of Taoist deities, Chinese coins on a string, bagua mirrors, and prismatic crystals are viewed by some as Chinese knickknacks. Others see them as welcome, if eclectic, additions to their home. My firm belief is that there is always a way to express the *intention* of a feng shui solution in any décor.

Yes, you *can* do it yourself! There are precious few situations so onerous that only a professional feng shui consultant can solve them. You must be willing to experiment, study like a fiend, and continually view your space with unemotional eyes. If you, the resident, are willing to put your emotions about objects and their arrangement aside, even briefly, you will surely be more effective in your feng shui applications. Finally, and I do believe, most importantly, there is intuition. Listen to it, cultivate it, act on it.

Chapter 1:

The Exterior

APPROACH

The physical environment around a dwelling can have a great impact on the residents. The outside is where energy (chi) finds you first. Put yourself in the position of a first-time visitor.

- Your house (or apartment) number should be very clearly visible. If it is appropriate, also have your name visible on the outside. An address number will benefit from having each digit slightly higher than the digit to its left. We read from left to right, so as we're reading our gaze is rising—our energy is also going up. It is especially important to have the address numbers slanted upward if the land behind the home slopes down.
- If you actually need a "No Trespassing" sign, use one that starts out saying "Private Property." That way "no" isn't the first word that's read.
- Brilliant red attracts chi energy more than any other color. Red objects (such as red flowering plants or plants in red glazed pots) near the street on each side of your driveway or walkway act as a stop sign to chi. "Stop, chi energy! Come in here!" Maximize the effect by repeating it near your front door. Realistic artificial plants can be used, but they must be replaced when they fade. Faded artificial plants do not attract chi energy and, in a sense, they repel it.
- A large object, such as a tree or electric pole, that is in a direct line between the street and your front door, represents an obstacle. I'm

a great lover of trees but this is not the right place for one. If the obstruction is not removable, there are three symbolic solutions: A small bagua mirror can be hung above your front door. This kind of mirror has an eight-sided frame with the different *I Ching* trigrams on each side. There is always a little hanging device on one side. Pay attention to that and keep that side up. It is considered to be powerful and is primarily for exterior use. Bagua mirrors are usually quite inexpensive and are available in any major Chinatown. Most, however, are cheaply made and can start to look faded and tacky after a while. That, in addition to the fact that they look a bit too hocus pocus for some tastes, may cause you to choose an alternative. Any mirror or very shiny, reflective, object (such as a brass doorknocker) will do. It is important that you feel comfortable with feng shui "cures" that you use. It is, after all, *your* home!

Another symbolic solution is to change the *purpose* of the "obstacle." It can become a "holder of an affirmation." To do that, you just put a real physical affirmation up in the tree. It could be a recovery coin that had a positive saying on it, or a small rock that had "love" or "peace" carved on it, or just a piece of metal foil that you emboss with words such as "look up, be well."

You could also plant a row of evergreen shrubs between the door and the "obstacle" to symbolize a buffer.

- If the pathway leading to your front door from the street or sidewalk is a very direct line, it needs to be tempered a bit. It's best if the chi meanders up to your front door instead of charging right in. One way to do this is by placing flowerpots (or other interesting outside ornaments) on the sides of the steps or pathway. Having the pots in a staggered pattern (not directly across from each other as in a formal arrangement) forces the visual energy to zigzag and therefore slow down. If the pots are themselves interesting or whimsical and each one is different, the solution will be even more effective. If you have a choice about where to locate the path to the front door, put it to the right of the front door (as you are standing at the street, looking toward your house.)
- A convex curve is the beginning of an angle pointing at you. It's not horribly bad, but being on the concave side of a curved road is always much better. Houses on the concave side are more protected than those on the convex side. See Fig. 1. Think of a sharp, curved knife, like a machete or scimitar. The convex side is sharp and dangerous. When cars move along the road, their lights shine onto the houses

on the convex side, not the concave side. Their lights are an uninvited intrusion. Homes at the very end of a cul-de-sac or T-intersection (see Fig. 2) also have this problem. It's time to plant a big fat hedge or put up a solid fence. If this isn't immediately feasible, then place a bagua mirror (see Glossary) outside your house facing the headlights. A convex mirror is an excellent alternative to a bagua mirror in this circumstance. You are basically saying "no" to that energy and sending it back.

Curved road

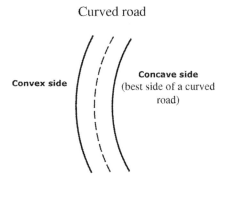

Fig. 1

Poison arrow to house

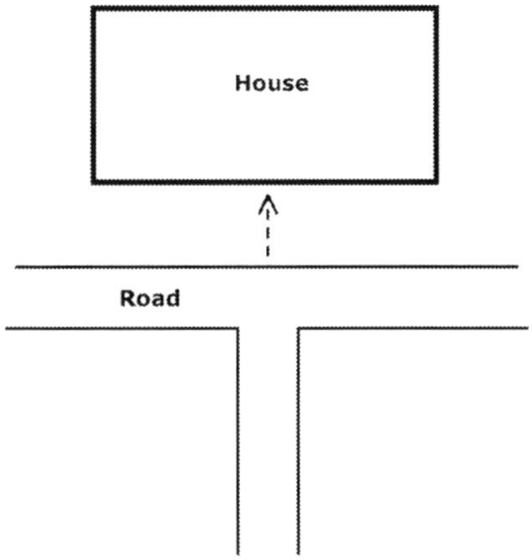

House

Road

Not a favorable location at a T-intersection.

Fig. 2

- When two driveways are *directly* opposite each other, they are in competition for luring chi energy. The larger one wins. If you cannot increase the size of your driveway, make it more noticeable. Use plants or ornamentation to make your driveway entrance stunning. Heads should turn toward your driveway. Use bright or noticeable sculpture, pottery, or plants (but not spiky-leaf plants). Lovely pavement on the driveway surface could remedy this situation very well. Even an arresting mailbox would work.

- Where the driveway meets the road it should be fairly level so energy rolls in evenly. If the driveway slopes down steeply toward the house, put plants along the driveway that have white flowers or leaves to lift the energy. Red flowers or leaves would also work. If the driveway slopes steeply uphill where it meets the road, energy coming to the house will roll back to the road before reaching the house. Put something reflective near the base of the driveway (where it meets the road). The reflective part should shine up the driveway, symbolically reflecting the energy back up your driveway. A small mirror or reflector will work, as will a silver garden gazing ball. The ball reflects in all directions and because *some* of it reflects up the driveway, it's fine.

- C-shaped driveways are not recommended because they are seen to have a strong cutting energy, portending divorce. See Fig. 3. Changing the driveway is ideal, but seldom feasible. Put a small crystal between the driveway and the house, or put a tiny mirror on the outside wall of the house down close to the ground, facing the driveway, and reflecting its energy away from your home. Full circle driveways are not a problem.

- It is best if the garage is not more prominent than the front door. If the garage is more prominent, it sends the energetic message that at least one of the people who lives there will be away from home a lot—life in the fast lane. Visually erase the garage by painting the garage doors and the trim around them the same color as the outside walls. Also work to make your front door area more noticeable. You can formalize it with matching planters on each side of the door, distinctive lighting, bright paint, windchimes, or whatever makes it stand out without looking outlandish.

C-shaped driveway

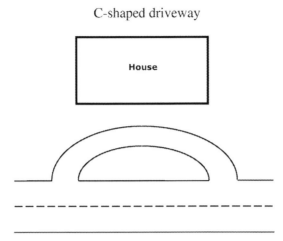

Fig. 3

- If there are stairs going up to your front door they need to have risers as well as treads. See Fig. 4. Stairs going up to back doors and side doors don't have to have risers. It's good for interior stairs to have risers, but it's not vital. Risers are the vertical parts of stairs that connect the treads. When you walk upstairs they are the part that your toes are pointing towards. They are rarely a structural necessity but energetically they are vital. If you can see right through the stairs, the chi energy is doing exactly what your eyes are doing. It is slipping through the open spaces and moving on. It is not rising up to your living space where it needs to go.

Risers

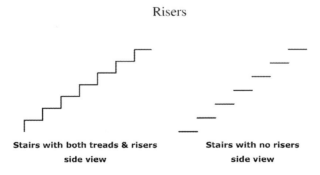

Stairs with both treads & risers   **Stairs with no risers**
side view   **side view**

Fig. 4

One woman could not add risers because she was a renter. Instead she stapled beautiful red oilcloth where the risers would have been. It was stunning and quickly effective.

There are certain kinds of cement stairs that resist any kind of riser addition. This is one of the very few instances where feng shui says, "You might want to move!" You are missing a huge percent of the chi energy that would otherwise be coming to you in your daily life. Moving is often not an option and if that's the case, do everything in your power to bring the visual energy continuously up the stairs. Matching red pots with matching plants on each side of each stair or a vine (live or artificial) trailing up along the banister railing are two possible solutions. An exterior fountain or windchime near the door would be good. Also do everything you can to visually emphasize your front door. You probably can't overdo it because the situation is somewhat dire and calls for a "say something" front door. Just be sure not to over-clutter the area.

If a condominium or apartment building has no risers on its stairs, but has an elevator, the stairs are not a big issue. The problem is when stairs with no risers are the only way to get to your front door.

FRONT DOOR

The front door is referred to as "the mouth of chi." The door that the architect intended to be the main entrance (where guests are usually received) is considered to be the front door for feng shui purposes. It doesn't matter whether or not another (side) door is used more frequently. If the front door has been completely blocked or nailed shut, then the secondary door becomes the new mouth of chi. In this instance, there are likely to be confused energies in the house. It would be best to go ahead and do whatever major remodeling it takes to totally erase the old front door and visually establish the new one. Other things to consider about the front door are:

- It should be the largest outside door—larger than any back or side doors.
- If there is also a screen (or storm) door, its hinges should be on the same side of the doorframe as those of the main door. This applies for any outside door. If this just isn't possible, hang a very small clear crystal up high in the space between the door and the screen door. The crystal symbolically disperses any confused energy between the two doors.

- Retractable screen doors on a spring are a nice idea, but the effect is usually a bit jarring.
- Door hinges should not squeak, and the door should open and close easily without catching or scraping on anything. This applies to any and every door.
- Front doors should open *inward*, inviting the chi energy inside. If they open outward, it can be seen as repelling the chi. Don't worry if a screen door opens outward; they usually have to.
- No cobwebs. I think the reason is obvious.
- Use your formal front door occasionally, even if it's not your main entrance.
- A single front door is best for most homes. Only very large homes should have a double front door, otherwise you may be asking for more than you can handle.

One of the fundamental aspects of a front door is that when it is closed, you should be able to have privacy. This also allows you to temper the chi flow. If the majority of the front door is clear glass, or if the areas immediately beside the front door are clear glass, chi can come and go any time, all the time—and it will! If someone standing outside your front door can see a lot of what is directly inside the door, you need some sheer curtains, either on the door or on the side windows next to it. On side windows, you may also use tall plants to provide privacy. Either option will still allow plenty of light to enter, which was undoubtedly the architect's intention.

If you're bold enough to paint your front door red, you're doing yourself a gigantic favor. If you can't bring yourself to paint it brilliant red, use whatever shade of red appeals to you. Only the outside of the door should be red. White or a dark color is more appropriate for that area *inside* the home.

I consulted for some folks with a bright yellow front door. They asked me if they should change the color to red. I told them that I had a hard time saying that, since yellow is my favorite color and the door was about as noticeable as it could be, but that technically, yes, red is the best color for a front door. They painted the door red and told me that within hours, thousands of dollars started pouring their way unexpectedly. There's nothing like red! However it can be difficult to get a saturated red color, without visible brushstrokes. Using a brown primer will make it so that fewer red coats are needed. An example of a deep rich red is "Fabulous Red" from Valspar—it's verging on an oxblood red.

FOREBODING OBJECTS

Threatening objects or poison arrows that aim at or loom toward your dwelling should be repelled with mirrors. Bagua mirrors are great, but any mirror will do. The use of outside (repelling) mirrors is both symbolic and quite real. It *is* best if the mirror is aimed exactly at the offending object. Some examples of threatening objects are:

- Large industrial smokestacks
- Large broadcasting towers
- Electrical transformers (fairly common)
- A building with a turret with a sharp cone top
- A cliff with large rocks that is close to and above your home
- A next-door neighbor's roof that is level with your window, with an excessive number of chimneys and vent fans
- Oversized church steeples
- A weedy, littered, vacant lot
- A dead tree
- A construction site
- The ocean or any severe land drop-off right next door
- A building with a large right angle pointed directly at your home. See Fig. 5. Google Earth is handy for checking whether or not a neighboring structure is "aimed" at you.

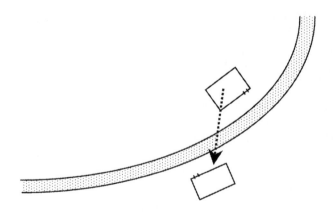

Poison Arrow from Another House

Fig. 5

If the object that you're repelling is quite large, a concave mirror will symbolically shrink it as well as repel it. A convex mirror is often best to repel the energy of a very busy road, like a freeway. When using a mirror outside to repel any form of harsh energy, try to locate the mirror near a door or window, as if it were guarding the opening. Doors and windows are the *vulnerable* areas of a home. (Thieves wouldn't just smash a hole in your wall to get in. They would come in through a door or window.)

In addition to the outside mirror, you might consider putting these things inside the window:

- A large plant coming up from below the window
- A crystal, windchimes, mobile, or stained glass in that window
- Sheer or lacy curtains
- A shoji screen
- Heavy drapes

Churches, especially those that are visually prominent with large steeples and crosses, are not considered to be good chi neighbors. Their exaggerated size, when viewed strictly as environmental landform, is often foreboding. Also, funerals are conducted there and many religious traditions believe that a person's spirit can remain in close proximity to their body for several weeks after death. If you have a door opening directly toward a church or cemetery next door, put a mirror (preferably a bagua mirror) over the outside of that door, facing away from your home.

If you live right next to a cemetery, keep a small light on at all times in front of an image that you think of as sacred.

Also, any power pole that has the metal rod steps for the repair worker to go up and down is called a "centipede pole" and doesn't bode well. The standard solution is to put a rooster statue or figurine somewhere on your property (inside or out), facing the pole. Chickens eat centipedes and roosters are considered to be the most powerful chickens.

Power lines that aren't seen are ideal, but that's not usually feasible, so the next consideration is the angle of the power line (or any line) where it enters the building. A very shallow angle is great, because it's as if the line were a blow to the building and the blow just glances off. If the angle is close to a right angle (90 degrees) it's as if the building received a direct hit. Symbolically reflect it back, but do so at a safe distance from the actual wire.

LAY OF THE LAND

The most ancient type of feng shui is the Landform School, predating even the Compass School. The energy of the lay of the land surrounding your dwelling can have a significant impact on your life. Proper landform around a home symbolizes protection, support, and awareness. The energy outside your home is represented by four animals:

- Green Dragon (masculine) on the right, if you are outside facing the front door
- White Tiger (feminine) on the left, if you are outside facing the front door
- Black Tortoise behind the house
- Red Phoenix (or Red Bird) in front of the house

The animals are considered archetypal and powerful. The shape and size of land features or other structures near your home is the energetic expression of these animals. The dragon and the tiger have potentially destructive energy. In the ideal situation they keep each other in check by being somewhat balanced. The dragon should technically be a bit higher than the tiger—3/5 for the dragon and 2/5 for the tiger. Large buildings or land features on either side of your home should seem balanced (when considering your house in the middle). If a large upward object on one side of your house is not balanced on the other side, then it's your job to bring about symbolic visual balance. "Symbolic" is the key word, because it is rarely feasible to create actual physical balance. A common solution is an exterior light pole in the side yard that needs the addition. Light is one of the most powerful expressions of chi energy and can work wonders! If nothing else, use a sculpture of the appropriate animal outside the house on the appropriate side.

The tortoise and phoenix are in proper energetic alignment when the land in front of your house slopes down, and the land behind your house slopes up. When you are standing inside your front door, looking out, the land should slope gently down toward the street or sidewalk. Behind your house the land should rise gently. That's the ideal. Now let's deal with the actual. Many houses do not have that landscape dynamic and something should be done to symbolically change the situation. If the land drops off dramatically behind your house, as is the case in many homes with "a great view," put a moving weathervane on top of your house to lift the energy upward. If you can add exterior lighting, do so with uplights, which shine upward onto the back of the building. Also, if it is possible, add a fountain outside your front door, with the water flowing toward the front door area or flowing 360 degrees, like an umbrella. This solution is subtle, but powerful. If the fountain flows constantly, it will continually oppose the dynamic set up by the lay of the land. In fact, it is *always* a good idea to have a water feature (a small pond or gentle fountain) in your front yard. It reinforces the feeling that the front yard is lower than the back yard, because water flows down and "collects" in your front yard.

Ideally the front door should be roughly in the center of the front wall, so that the home has a balanced energy. If the front door is way off to the right side of the front wall (as you stand outside looking at the front door), there isn't adequate room for the dragon energy. To supplement this energy, you could place a dragon statue outside somewhere to the right of the front door. Any masculine image would actually work, and this is especially recommended if the occupant is looking for a boyfriend. If the front door is way off to the left (as you stand out side looking at the front door), the tiger energy is disempowered. Put a tiger statue outside to the left of the door. If you're looking for a girlfriend, put a feminine image there.

Chapter 2:

Chi Flow

Chi is just the Chinese name for what is perhaps the most basic thing in the universe—energy. Do not think of it as some ghostly, amorphous thing. You, yourself, are a high expression of chi energy. When something gets your attention, chi energy is being drawn there. Your clue is the fact that you noticed it. Your neck muscles moved so that you could turn your head. Your eye muscles moved so that you could look toward that "something." Energy was required for those muscles to move. Madison Avenue is expert at attracting chi energy, even though the advertisers probably don't think of it that way. Light, movement, and sound are primary attractors of chi. This is why prismatic crystals and water fountains are recommended so often in feng shui.

It is not difficult to determine how chi flows within a building. If there are places where you are able to move quickly (such as a long straight hallway), chi energy is speeding right along. When this happens the chi is packing a punch and is not considered to be very healthy. If there are places where your movement is very encumbered (such as corners that are overly filled with furniture or objects) most likely chi energy is stagnating there.

Long straight hallways conduct chi energy too quickly. If the hall is wide enough, put one or more narrow tables along the walls. If multiple tables are used, stagger them on opposite sides. This causes the chi to zigzag and thereby slow down. If the hall is too narrow for tables, use pictures, mirrors, or wall sculptures. Use rugs to slow the energy, but be aware that our eyes automatically follow straight lines, so be sure that the pattern on the rug isn't long straight lines going the length of the hall. That would just guide the energy to go fast. If it is possible to add lighting, do so with splashes of light playing on the walls. Make the hall so interesting and pleasant that one is tempted to linger there, as in an art gallery. If the art is tactile and one is tempted to touch it, that's even better. Feel free to hang mobiles, windchimes, or crystals from the ceiling. If doors are left open or ajar along the hallway, this will cause chi to flow into those rooms rather than just zooming down the hall. Keep doors to bathrooms and closets closed, however.

Do not let anything accumulate behind a door in such a way that the door cannot open to its fullest. The door is what allows the energy to enter the room. To whatever degree it is blocked, that amount of potential is not reaching your life. When a door opens, chi can flow in smoothly or it can sometimes get disturbed. A wall that confronts you as soon as you've stepped into a space is jarring to chi. It will help greatly to put a picture or mirror on that wall. The picture should be one with visual depth, such as a landscape. If the wall that confronts you has a door that is almost, but not quite, directly in front of you, the effect is disturbing in a slightly different way. It would be best to hang a crystal in the hall between the two doors.

Drapes that are very long and puddle on the floor affect chi in a good way. If the "pile of fabric" on the floor looks good—not dusty and dirty—it catches the eye, and the strong vertical line of the drape then pulls the eye (and the chi) up. It is very healthy to cause chi to rise up like that, and even regular floor-length drapes will work fine.

LOSS OF CHI

Notice how your eyes move when you step inside a room and are looking around. If there are things that get your attention, that's where chi is going first. A very common problem is a window or glass door directly opposite the entrance door. It is almost impossible not to look outside. That is exactly what chi does. It makes a beeline out of your place and it's gone! It can be miles away in an instant and it ain't coming back! Modern design often says let the view be the most important thing. Feng shui says that if the view rules, the chi (attentive energy) of most people is going out of your home—to the view. This lets you know that chi energy in general is vanishing out that window. People may bemoan the loss of a great view, but it is often best to be close to a window before the fullest view is appreciated—on a porch or deck is preferred.

The most effective solution to this problem is to create a "show stopper" within your space. Place something that competes with the view in front of, or very close to, the view window or door. This can be as simple as a stunning orchid in bloom (for a small window) or (for a large expanse of glass) it may need to be something like a sculpture that grabs your attention and won't let go. However long your attention is held inside your space is valuable time. It gives chi time to flow around the room and fill up the corners. Remember that the color red acts as a stop sign to chi energy as no other color can. The effect you want to create is, "What a lovely orchid! Oh, and what a great view!" Let the view be a fabulous bonus that is discovered *after* the attention has stayed inside for a moment. Sometimes a moment is all you can hope for, but that's enough, as long as the dynamic that is created is *first* inside, *then* outside. Other suggestions to hold chi in the room are:

- A crystal or windchimes hung in a direct line between the entrance and the view.
- A bagua mirror over the view window or door. This is one of about three times when it's okay (and advisable) to put a bagua mirror inside a house. Any time that I recommend a bagua mirror, please realize that *any* mirror will work.
- A windowbox can be perfect in certain situations. It stops the visual energy right outside the room, and draws it back from a very distant and commanding view.

Overly large windows (i.e., walls of glass) and windowpanes that meet exactly in a corner allow chi energy to slide right out of your life. They also do not allow you any control of the chi pouring into your life. Consider using sheer drapes or stained glass panels, both of which go well with modern décor. If the curtains are very "gauzy" they should probably be white or off-white to avoid coloring the light in the room.

You've probably gotten the idea by now that chi behaves somewhat like moving water or wind. This is why drains are considered to be a problem. Chi wanders into your bathroom, finds several convenient drains, and flows right out of your house. Don't let it happen! Cover your drains to whatever degree is feasible. If a drain cannot have a stopper over it, then a haircatching strainer is the next best thing. It at least reduces the visible size of the drain. Be sure the shower curtains or doors are closed in such a way that the drain is not visible. It is important to avoid mildew, so they can be left somewhat open for air circulation, if necessary. Just be sure that the drain itself isn't visible unless you poke your head into the shower area. The toilet lid must stay down at all times when the toilet is not in use. A lot of people seem to resist this rule. All I can say is, "Get over it and get used to it!" It is so important—it is a #1 rule! It is also best to keep the bathroom doors closed, or only slightly ajar (if air circulation is an issue). Mirrors on the outside of bathroom doors are almost always a good idea. They work in two ways: by reflecting and repelling the chi and keeping it from going into the bathroom in the first place, and by sealing off the body waste energy of the bathroom from the rest of the house. The silvering on the back of the mirror has a symbolic sealing effect. If the bathroom door opens directly into a kitchen it is *vital* that the door stay closed and be mirrored. Foods to eat and body waste to expel are opposite energies and their vibrations need to be quite separate. Within a kitchen, all drains should be closed or at least have strainers.

If there are sticks in your house (any kind of sticks: lumber, walking sticks, driftwood, or dried stick arrangements) that are somewhat vertical and are touching the floor, remove them. When chi encounters those sticks it is conducted down and out. It is especially bad when the sticks are in the Fortunate Blessings area.

If stairs to the upper floor are directly in front of (and facing) the entrance door, the chi may not stay inside your house. Imagine the chi bounding into your house, heading directly up the stairs then just rolling right back out your front door. That's pretty much what happens. It probably does not happen if the stairs are more than approximately 12 feet from the door. In that case the chi has plenty of time to "get curious" about the lower floor and begin to circulate there. Stairs that are closer than 12 feet to (and directly facing) the front door would benefit from having a large potted plant at the bottom. The plant form should be uprising, not drooping. A very large floor vase or umbrella stand could also work, symbolically catching the chi that is trying to leave. Putting a bagua mirror inside above the door is also recommended. This is another instance when it is okay to put a bagua mirror inside.

It's good (but not vital) for interior stairs to have risers. If you absolutely cannot install risers of any sort, then you need to give chi a reason to want to go upstairs. It is essential that chi circulate throughout all of your home. Do whatever is in your power to create a vibrant visual flow up to the next floor. Do not forget the power of bright color.

Stairs in the center of the house are not a good idea according to feng shui, especially spiral stairs. Spiral stairs in the center are called "corkscrew through the heart." Stairs are considered spiral if they curve around enough so that some steps are directly above other steps. They're cute, but they can easily cause a slight disorientation. If you have them, you probably cannot do anything about them, so the best idea is to bless them, hang a crystal, windchimes, or mobile over them and go on with your life. If possible have an upward-shaped plant somewhere near the base of the stairs, to symbolically lift energy.

CLUTTER

Clutter has an immediate and drastic stagnating effect on chi. Places with dusty unused clutter that has been around for decades are totally lacking in healthy energy. If your clutter is severe, take some severe measures. It is blocking your progress in life and affecting your health. Everything you own (even if it is in storage elsewhere) is connected to you energetically. If it isn't used on a regular basis, it's holding you back and weighing you down. Feng shui emphasizes purging clutter because the effect is so immediately liberating. The Universe cannot pour fresh new energy into your "cup" if it's constantly full of old stuff. It is virtually impossible for a cluttered place to be a clean place, and cleanliness is vital to feng shui. When it comes to reaching your potential, a dirty house is directly and strongly working against you. Faced with clutter overload, there are two preferred areas to begin clearing the clutter—near the entrance door and in the two back corners of the room. If it is your intention to declutter, the effect will be much more resounding in those areas. Clutter itself is a vicious cycle, and decluttering near the entrance of a room breaks the stagnant inertia so that fresh energy can begin to flow more easily into the space, assisting the organizing process. Do not let clutter be reflected in a mirror because it is doubled.

The key to successful decluttering is to be able to pull yourself out of the emotional attachment. Here are some tips that might be helpful:

- As you are going through your objects, rate them: 1, 2, or 3. 1 is for things that you use consistently or love too much to even consider getting rid of. 3 is for things that you are sure you can part with. 2 is for things that you can't decide about. With this technique, the things that you can't decide about don't bog you down and drain your energy. They just go into a pile, quick and easy, and you can come back to that pile when you have the energy. That way decisions get made and at least some stuff can be eliminated immediately. Work away at the number 2 pile a bit at a time.

- Pick up an object and as you look at it say to yourself, "If I saw this in a store right now, would I buy it?" This technique is especially effective for gifts that you never liked in the first place. I hope I'm not the first person to tell you that just because someone gave you something, that is not a reason you should keep it. Keep it if you really, really, like it—otherwise, let it go (hopefully into a system of reuse).

- Get together a group of objects, and then divide the group in half according to which objects are of more monetary value. Keep the ones that are worth more and part with the ones that are worth less. This technique is appalling to some, but it sure does the trick of emotionally detaching. It probably shouldn't be the sole technique that anyone uses, and shouldn't be used on all objects.

Any professional organizer will tell you that "because it may come in handy someday" is definitely not a good reason to keep an object. Conceivably anything could come in handy someday. A feng shui consultant will say exactly the same thing, but for a different reason. If you are keeping an object just "because it may come in handy someday" you are saying to yourself (and the Universe) that when and if you *do* need that object, you won't have the means to obtain it. So by hanging onto it you are truly, if unintentionally, promoting your own poverty consciousness. Hanging onto the objects can also stifle hope, thereby making deep peace more elusive in your life.

The sustainable economies of the future will have to be based on reuse. Otherwise the planet cannot support this vast number of humans. When you let go of items that you are not currently using, you release them into systems of reuse, and are helping to preserve resources and the environment. Likewise, try to stop shopping—no more indiscriminate consumption (buying an object, *then* trying to figure where to put it). It's good to remember that the word consumption used to refer to a disease. Clutter doesn't have two legs and walk into you house on its own. *Somebody* has to bring it in; don't let that person be you. Just learn a new habit. Feng shui is sometimes about doing things once, and sometimes it's about changing a habit.

Interior objects are functional and/or decorative. Do not over-decorate your home with nonfunctional objects—things that just sit there and look nice. It is quite important to be able to detach (emotionally and physically) from objects that are basically dragging you down. You have an opportunity to make your life better by letting go of any of these things that may be around your home:

- Representations of bodies with missing body parts or representations of ruins.
- Artwork with images that seem threatening, dire, or depressing. I consulted for a woman who had a painting (that a friend had made) of a woman with an anxious expression. Behind the woman in the painting was a dark hooded figure that had its hands (with long sharp fingernails) on the woman's shoulders. This was the first image that my client saw when she entered her home. I told her it was inappropriate in her home, and her mother, who was also attending the consultation, practically jumped with joy and said, "How about the one in the living room? I don't like the one in the living room either." Since the only problem with the painting in the living room was that it was obviously amateur, I told her it could stay.
- Things that are "too unfriendly" poison-arrow-wise.

- Things that physically don't fit the space. Move them or get rid of them. Any time the base of an object protrudes over the edge of a table or shelf, the message is "imbalance" or "lack of support."
- Objects that are waiting for repair. It is quite okay to have things that need a bit of repair work, but it is *best* to store them out of sight.
- Glass tabletops (unless they are rimmed) and glass shelves (unless they are over head height).
- "Too much stuff," which can often lead to a seemingly insurmountable messiness. Sometimes "too much stuff" simply means that every surface is over-decorated. Feng shui's view of having too much stuff is that you are only hurting yourself. Greed brings with it a karmic reward, causing your life to seem too busy—no time to enjoy life. Too much stuff equals unnecessary burdens—a simple and accurate equation. If, as time goes by, you find that time seems to be speeding up—I guarantee that you will benefit by getting rid of many objects that you don't regularly *use*. Pare down your life to things you use and/or love.

We humans are adept at making things, and have been doing so for many millennia. Don't be surprised that when you get rid of objects that aren't helping in your life, better stuff comes your way, as you are also more attuned to noticing it. Things around you *are influencing you*.

To make any home more visually peaceful, eliminate "brand-name clutter." Carefully cut labels from cushions and towels, and save them if you think you might ever need them. (In case you don't know, a tag on a cushion or pillow that says, "Do not remove under penalty of law" applies only while the store owns it.) Remove barcode, brand name, and price stickers. Don't leave those out in the home to be looked at. They're too eye-catching and within a home, can represent chaos. Labels are fine in stores, but once you own an item remove its label, if the item will be in view. Thereby your home will be more visually peaceful. Anytime your eyes notice a written brand name in you home, find a way to cover it or put it away. If you are buying new items, try to get toilets without brand names, water faucets without brand names, et cetera. Get things that just do their job, not things that are constantly touting their brand. So what if it's expensive and the name is what proves it—don't be that shallow. Give your brain a rest.

Another way to give your brain a rest is by culling the audio advertisements in your space, which means less commercial radio and television. The most peaceful sounds are nature or silence. They are what give you your own mental space. Music is fine, but if it has lyrics in a language that you understand, it's claiming your mind. There's a time and a place for everything, but if you want a more peaceful life, have fewer lyrics in your space.

EMPOWERED POSITIONS

As chi enters a room, it brings with it the aspect of that which is new or just coming into your life. On a practical level, if you can see the main door to a room from the place where you spend the most time in that room, you've got an advantage. If you can't, you've got a disadvantage. When you can see the doorway (without moving your head more than 90 degrees) you've empowered yourself and strengthened your own natural ESP. When you can't see the doorway, you've disempowered yourself and set yourself up for surprises that you may be unprepared for. Things will seem to come out of "left field." These are the places where it matters the most:

Bed

Your bed is the most important place in your home because on an average people spend a third of their lives there. The more time you spend in a particular place or room, the more resonance it has in your life. There are rules upon rules when it comes to placing a bed. Being able to see the doorway is just one of them. Others include:

- Don't place the bed so that the head is on a wall with a toilet on the other side. If this must happen, at least place a small mirror behind the bed, facing the wall, to repel the toilet vibration. The mirror does not have to be visible. The mirror is hanging backwards but it will not look strange because it will not be seen.
- Don't place your bed (especially your head) right next to a window, unless the window is several feet above the bed.
- Don't place a bed in the direct pathway of the door. If you have no alternative, place a screen or large plant between the door and the bed.
- Dead bodies are generally removed from a room feet first, which causes some people to believe that it is unfortunate to sleep with one's feet pointed directly at the bedroom door. It's called the "coffin position," and your full body is in the pathway of the swath of strong energy from the door. Fig. 6 shows the coffin position and Fig. 7 shows what is *not* a coffin position, because the bed is not in line with the door.

- If a couple sleeps in the bed, it is important that one person does not have to crawl over the other to get out of bed. Try to have at least eighteen inches on either side of the bed for walking around. Allow at least eighteen inches *anywhere* you expect people to pass by, otherwise you are pinching chi energy.

Bed in coffin position

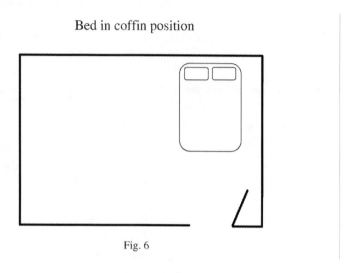

Fig. 6

Bed *not* in coffin position

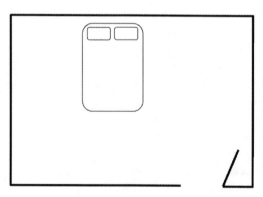

Fig 7

When all these rules are applied, it sometimes leaves only one obvious place for the bed. But sometimes there is no ideal place for the bed, in which case a mirror may be needed so that the door is easily visible. Locate the mirror so that occupants of the bed can just open their eyes and easily see the door.

Mirrors in the bedroom are loved by some feng shui teachers and loathed by others. All agree that it's fine to use a mirror to see the door. A wall of mirrored closet doors can definitely make for disturbed sleep for some people. If that seems to be the case with you, put up a rod over the mirrors, hang curtains, and close them at night.

Desk

Your desk can be a very important area, depending upon its frequency of use and what type of work is done there. Running a business from your desk causes it to be extremely important.

Once again there are a lot of rules about positioning a desk. There should not be a window directly behind your back. A wall gives you support, and that symbol translates into the effectiveness of the work that is done at the desk. If a window is absolutely the only option, it needs to be well screened. Shoji screens are ideal because they feel architectural. Shades and curtains are okay, but blinds can be problematic depending on how they are positioned. They need to be fairly well closed if they are behind your back. If shelving is behind your back, it needs to be enclosed within doors so that you don't normally see the actual shelves. If this isn't feasible, put a real "from the earth" crystal (not a prismatic lead crystal) on each shelf, from the floor to top-of-head height. Shelves that are higher than head height are problematic for a different reason. Their height is said to cause neck problems. Blinds and shelves can send out poison arrows, stabbing you in the back. There is not universal agreement about whether a desk should be freestanding in the room or be adjacent to a wall. Those who like it to be adjacent to a wall cite the concern that the desk is in a position similar to a coffin at a funeral, where it is possible to walk all the way around it. Others view the actual energetics of the desk and say that realistically it gives you more options and therefore you will *have* more options—not bad at all.

You need to be able to see the doorway from your desk without moving your head more than 90 degrees. If you are looking at a computer monitor and someone is quietly standing in the doorway waving, you need to know about it. If you must place a desk so that you cannot see the doorway, you will need a mirror so that if there is movement in the doorway, you will instantly know about it. Gooseneck shaving mirrors are a solution because they can easily be positioned correctly. Some people put mirrors right on their computer monitors because that's where they are looking most of the time. Small convex mirrors can be attached with double-sided foam tape. It may require a bit of extra tape on one side to position it so that the doorway is exactly in view.

I feng shui'd the offices of a computer software consulting company, with a very egalitarian corporate culture. There were no separate offices and the CEO's desk was much too close to the reception area. I couldn't get him to change that or even to locate his desk so that he could easily see toward the door (sometimes I wonder why people call me). The best I could do was to put a convex mirror on a walnut bookend right next to his monitor so he could see the door area. When a new employee was hired the CEO's desk area got reconfigured and once again he could not see toward the door. As things were shifted around two file boxes got put in the trash. Those boxes contained all the records of all the work he had done in the last two years. You see why I say don't have your back to the door!

Another time I consulted for the CEO of one of the largest Internet shopping sites. Her office had a spectacular view of the San Francisco Bay, and that's what she looked at from her desk. I had a hard time telling her that it would be best to turn her desk so that the door would be part of her view. There was no way she was going to turn that desk, so I immediately suggested a convex mirror, realizing that it would look rather out-of-place in her stunning office. She shook her head and then I said, "How about some rounded reflective object that lets you see behind you, like a vase?" She smiled and said, "A mercury glass vase—I'll have no trouble finding that. I'm a great shopper." I grinned and said, "I bet you are!"

Stove

The stove is an undeniably powerful object. If left unattended at the wrong time, it could destroy your house. When working at the stove, you need to be able to see the doorway. If it is not already set up that way, you probably cannot move it, and once again a mirror is needed. The mirror should be placed so that the cook is aware of any movement in the doorway. Mirrors behind a stove are an area of disagreement among feng shui teachers. Some modern teachers say that a mirror behind the stove is always a good idea because it symbolically doubles the burners on the stove and thereby suggests that you are able to feed more people, hinting at more prosperity. Traditional feng shui teachers say this is a gross misreading of a basic rule. The rule is that it's a great idea to have a mirror reflecting the dining room table because when the bounty on the table is "doubled" it is beneficial to your prosperity. They use the phrase "fire at heaven's gate" to refer to mirrors behind the stove, and say that it portends accidents in the family. Common sense says that a mirror behind a stove is going to require a lot of cleaning; otherwise it's going to look bad. My suggestion is to put a mirror behind a stove only when it is needed to see the doorway, and try to angle it so that the burners are not reflected.

Also make sure that the mirror shows your head fully, if it shows any part of your body. My usual suggestion is to keep a shiny, dome-shaped, stainless steel water kettle on the stove. It serves the same purpose as the mirror because of its reflective quality, and it looks quite natural.

Remember those three items: the bed, the desk, and the stove. They are acknowledged by all feng shui schools as having great importance *because they can orient your awareness* of what will be happening in your life. The psychic result could be described as a gentle harmonizing with your intuition. You are willingly setting yourself up for reality. You are *aware* of the entrance and are feeding that information to your intuition. Before one moon cycle (about 28 days) some part of you will have breathed a sigh of relief. Your intuition will be more grounded in reality and you will be more inclined to listen to it. Your deepened bond with your intuition is one of feng shui's greatest gifts.

Other Positions

Empowered positions are sometimes called "command positions" and besides the bed, the desk, and the stove, several other areas can have a very strong impact:

- Most people have a dining table, even though it may not be used for every meal. Wherever you sit down to eat, you need to be able to see the doorway (and preferably not have your back to a window). Wall mirrors can sometimes help and they have the advantage of symbolically doubling the prepared food on the table. In a couple, if one person's back is always to the door, and the other person always faces the door, this sets up a dynamic that will not be healthy for the longevity of the relationship. Switch around occasionally. If there is a problem of strife (involving children) in your home, be aware of who sits where when the family eats together. The adults should always sit in the seats where they have the best view of the door. This practice will support their parenting skills. If one of the children is overactive at the table, that child's back should definitely be to the door. You can bring more harmony to dinner parties by using this principle. Place the more shy and reserved people so that they can see the door. Place your most outgoing guests with their back to the door.
- If you have a favorite lounge chair or preferred sitting spot for reading or television viewing, you need to be able to see the doorway from that place. Either rearrange the furniture or place a mirror or silver gazing ball so that you can see the doorway.

- The tub is important, but only if you take a lot of tub baths—three or four times a week. On most tubs, the end away from the faucet is the head end. That end should be farthest from the door. Then you can see the door. If your back is to the door, you will need a mirror above the faucet area, showing the door. Suction mirrors for tile walls are common. If you take long, soaking baths for the sake of relaxing, the mirror will allow the relaxation to reach deeper. Be sure not to use multiple mirror tiles because they break up your reflection.

POISON ARROWS

In any of those five important places—bed, desk, stove, dining chair, lounge chair (and possibly tub), it is best not to be in a direct line with the doorway, because the chi often comes into a room with a lot of force. This is especially the case when the door is at the end of a long hallway. When chi meets up with very straight lines the results can be quite troublesome. The energy is then referred to as poison arrow energy (sometimes called secret arrow or *sha* or *shar* in Chinese). When that energy encounters a place where you spend a lot of time, you need to pay attention and do something about the situation. You are being adversely affected, and because it happens repeatedly your health could suffer. It is to your benefit to know what is pointing at you. These are the main causes of poison arrows:

- Open beams crossing directly over your bed, a favorite chair, where you stand when cooking at the stove, or any spot where you spend a good bit of time. If they are fake beams, remove them and be happy, but if they are structural, painting them is often the best option. Make them visually disappear by painting them the same color as the ceiling. If there's some reason that keeps you from painting, you can make them energetically friendlier by hanging a crystal or windchimes over the place where you spend time. Some feng shui teachers say that the best way to deal with these beams is by hanging a pair of bamboo flutes on them. There is a special way to hang the flutes. Use red ribbon to hang the flutes at a forty-five-degree angle with mouthpieces down and toward the walls. It is as if someone were playing the flute and the energy of the breath coming through was lifting the beam. The flutes are at opposite ends of the beam. Sometimes a beam lends itself to having a plant (real or artificial) trail along it and perhaps twine around it. It is especially important that the lower part of the beam be covered. Another solution is to attach beautiful fabric to the ceiling, covering the beam. Uplighting, such as a wall sconce or torchière, can counter the effect of the beam if placed directly under it. A mirrored tabletop under the beam would also work, or even a mirror coaster on a table, as long as it's directly under the beam.

- Ceiling fans are to be praised for their aid in air circulation, but that doesn't mean that they are healthy to sit or sleep directly under. They add pressure to your life because they resemble a hand pressing down on you. They need to match the ceiling color in all situations. Sometimes this is as easy as unscrewing the blades and flipping them over. At other times, there is no choice but to paint or replace the blades. If it is possible to hang a crystal from the center of the ceiling fan, do so.

- Adjustable louvers are common in modern life. They come in many forms:
  —Venetian blinds
  —Mini blinds
  —Vertical blinds (the worst)
  —Plantation shutters
  —Jalousie windows

  They all have the potential of aiming poison arrows. The main thing about them is to be sure that they are not adjusted to aim at you as if they were blades, ready to symbolically "slice" you. If you are just passing by them there is not a problem, but if they are aimed where you spend a lot of time be sure to adjust them.

- Open shelves are also considered to act as blades. Consider the edges of the shelves to be similar to knife edges, and don't let them be pointed at you. Open shelves behind your back are a very bad idea, especially when you are sitting at a desk. Move them or cover them! If you cannot do that, put a real earth crystal on each shelf. Shelves that are an inch and a half thick or thicker do not have a slicing energy. You can add a lip to the shelf (extending down from the top of the shelf board), which makes the shelf look thicker.

- One of the worst poison arrow generators is furniture with sharp right angles. If the angle is *well* rounded or if it is larger than 90 degrees, no problem is created. However, if the angle is sharp, and 90 degrees or less, you've got the beginning of an "arrowhead" and it's time to move furniture or replace it. The simplest way of blocking the effect of a poison arrow is to place a large object between its origin and its target. If none of these choices is feasible, there is one final option. Cover the offending angle with a plant, or drape something over it, such as a tablecloth. To see the exact path of this kind of poison arrow, divide the offending angle in half and follow where it points. See Fig. 8. It is quite specific and if it points out into a space that you only walk by or rarely sit in, it isn't hurting you. The exception to that rule is: When this type of poison arrow (coming from a sharp right angle) is pointing directly at someone entering a room, it is subliminally saying "no" to them, and it is also saying no to chi energy. People working in offices should be aware of potential poison arrows from large file cabinets. If the cabinet can't be moved, your can cut a very long pie slice out of a wooden dowel. See Fig. 9. Paint it the same color as the cabinet and glue it on. Bedside tables are truly one of the worst offenders in this category of poison arrows. Time after time I use my finger to draw a line across someone's bedspread to show where a poison arrow is going. The client gasps and says, "Oh, my God, that's where my arthritis is!" or "That crosses right over my heart. That's my main health problem." or "That points to my breast and I've had breast cancer." If you don't do anything else about the side tables, at least cover them (with a towel or handkerchief or whatever) when you go to bed for the night—every night. If you have extra pillows on your bed, you can use those pillows to stuff between the poison arrow and your bed. A bed with a post at each corner can have four poison arrows if those posts have right angles. Use a canopy or pillows to buffer the sleeper from the harsh energy.

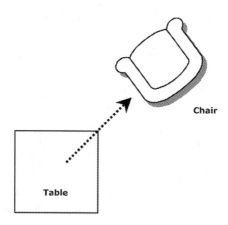

Poison Arrow from Furniture

Fig. 8

Fig. 9

- A sharp right angle can jut into a room where two walls come together. If that angle points to an entrance or anyplace where a person spends a lot of time, the corner should be rounded (bullnosed) or buffered with fabric or a tall object such as a plant.
- Doors that are partially open can aim a poison arrow out into the room. Wherever the door is pointing in the room is where the poison arrow is pointing. See Fig. 10. The solution to this, of course, is to open or close your doors a bit more fully.

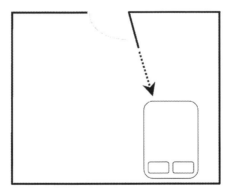

Poison Arrow from Door

Fig. 10

- Ceiling light fixtures sometimes have finials that point down sharply. Do not sit under them, and if possible replace them with more blunted finials.
- When doing deskwork, don't let sharp pencils or pens be pointing at you.
- If you regularly sit at a dining table with a line where two sections of the table come together, try to move your chair so the line doesn't point at you. If you can't move your chair, use a tablecloth or even a placemat to cover the line.
- Horizontally-displayed wine bottles should not have their cork end pointed at where someone enters the room or where they sit. That end of the wine bottle looks too gun-like. Move the wine rack or flip the bottles around, so their back end is toward the room.

ATTRACTING CHI

Just as there are techniques for keeping chi out of places where you don't want it (e.g. drains) there are lots of ways to summon chi energy to certain areas of your home. For example, it is generally a great idea to attract chi to a Fortunate Blessings area.

There is an easy and very effective way to conduct chi where you want it to go. It's a trick that designers commonly use, though probably without considering its feng shui ramifications. Angle your rug. The fringe on one end of a rug says, "Step onto this end and walk off the opposite end." When you have studied the bagua map (in the next chapter) and want to emphasize a certain area, rugs are a great way to do it. Just as they direct traffic, they direct chi. Because they are walked on they have the quality of being fundamental, like a foundation. Angled rugs are not perfect for every situation, but they are usually fairly easy to move. Consider trying it for a week or so to see how you like it. It makes a room more alive and dynamic, but it is certainly not for every rug and every room. Many rooms feel better with a more formal rug arrangement. Note that wherever rugs are they should have pads beneath them—to stabilize them and to preserve them. A rug pad can extend the life of a rug by hundreds of years!

Angled rugs and furniture are not an area of universal agreement in feng shui. Some teachers declare than angling things leads to chaotic thinking. This has not been my experience. What I have seen is that angling things indicates that the residents make their own rules in life. The walls are there to hold up the ceiling, and nothing more. They do not dictate the furniture arrangement. Realize that you can use basic design principles to your advantage. Visual energy is moved when the eye is moved in a certain way by a line or through repetition. Artists do this in pictures and it is exactly the same thing moving chi energy through your home.

Remember this: Anything that attracts your attention is attracting chi energy, because *you* are an example of chi energy. You notice light, color, motion, sound, and fragrance (and especially combinations of these such as glitter, shimmer, and iridescence) and therefore they are attracting chi. Specific ways to attract chi include:

Prismatic Crystals

These are *clear* lead glass crystals, usually made in Austria. You can use natural crystals from the earth, but they should be completely clear and capable of making rainbows in full sunlight. The round disco-ball type is often recommended. If sunlight actually reaches the crystal, you may want to use the kind that is octagon-shaped. They are unsurpassed for throwing large brilliant colors. The best octagon crystals have only a few facets (cuts) that are fairly large. See Fig. 11. Some octagon crystals are recently on the market that are quite inferior. They have many small facets radiating from the center like a sunburst, and do a very poor job of making colors over a large distance. See Fig. 12.

This octagonal crystal has large facets and makes large, brilliant rainbows.

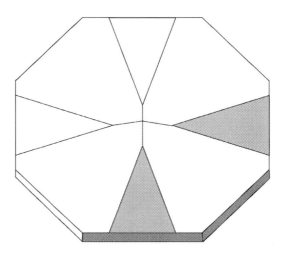

Fig. 11

This octagonal crystal has too many small facets
and will not make good rainbows.

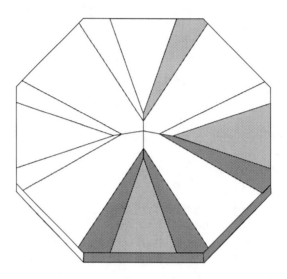

Fig. 12

Crystals work in a fairly obvious way. As they move, light glints off of their facets, and they can make rainbows. The more attention-getting, the more effective. Large is often best, but feel free to use any kind. Any time a crystal is used as a feng shui solution, it is important that you hold the intention of its use in your mind when hanging it. I recommend saying your intention out loud—something like, "I am hanging this crystal to disperse energy." Some people believe that the cure becomes even more effective if the crystal is hung from a red thread cut to nine inches or a multiple of nine inches. The crystal can then be hung at any height that seems good do you. It is the thread cutting that is symbolic. In my own practice, I always use clear monofilament (fishing line) to avoid a garish look. The crystal itself is a powerful enough cure (in my opinion) without the addition of red or special numbers.

Windchimes

Windchimes are best if placed where a breeze can actually touch them, but don't let that stop you from putting them anywhere inside your house. If they get no breeze, just touch them occasionally to enjoy their sound. Windchimes are valued for their shape as well as their sound. The ideal shape is hollow vertical pipes, which are commonly available. Their energy is especially uplifting. Windchimes that are pieces of glass clinking together are not recommended. Door harps are an underused feng shui enhancement. See Fig. 13. They can go on the back of any door to make a charming melody, similar to a dulcimer, when the door is moved. They are tunable, and be sure to tune them well. "My dog has fleas" is the standard tune when there are four strings.

Fig. 13

Fountains

It is hard to beat a fountain for attracting chi, because they make both sound and visual movement. One of the few places where they are not recommended is the Fame area (see Bagua Map in the next chapter), because the proper element there is Fire. Fire and water are big-time opposites! Also avoid putting water features in the center of your home—Earth is the element there. It's best if fountains are kept going all the time, and if that can't happen, then use a fountain that has some water visible even when the motor is turned off. When there is no water visible, the fountain is basically working against you by giving the message of "dried up." Any fountain should be kept going more than twelve hours per day. Solar fountains that only work when it's sunny are fine if there's always water visible.

When buying a fountain in a store, be sure to put your ear right next to the motor when it is running. If the motor sound is very noticeable, you'll probably find it much more so in the quiet of your home. Many motors are almost silent, but the ones that make noise are irritating when what you wanted was water sound. Another thing to consider with fountains is the splash factor and what that may mean to nearby surfaces. A fountain motor should be turned up fairly high so that plenty of splash sound is heard. If the basin that catches the water is deep and curves up and over a bit, there will be little or no oversplash, no matter how rapidly the fountain is running. Also, something like a stone tabletop is not going to be harmed by some water oversplash, but a wood tabletop should be used with caution to avoid damage to its finish.

Some fountains have a light bulb beneath the water, illuminating the water. This is mixing two opposing elements, Fire and Water, and is not recommended. Lava lamps may be thought of in the same way.

Plants

Healthy, living, plants are obviously better than artificial ones. They don't just attract chi energy, they *are* chi energy! However, realistic artificial plants are a fine substitute in areas that are too dark or unreachable, or if the resident isn't knowledgeable about proper living plant care, or is gone for long periods of time. Feng shui cautions against plants that have the ability to hurt you, such as cactus with spines, sharp leaves like yucca, and plants with thorns. The natural defense mechanism that the plant has evolved is generally for the purpose of keeping living beings away from it. That kind of vibration within your house ("stay away") is never appropriate.

Dried Plants

It is best not to use dried plants unless they are less than six months old. They are dead, and their energy reads "dead." The sap is gone from them, and they begin to rob you of your vitality and hold you in the past. Some people like to keep dried flowers from sentimental occasions. It is truly not a good idea. Strew the petals onto the ground and let them go back to the earth. Fresh energy, with your name on it, has been waiting in the wings for that moment. Artificial plants do not have this characteristic since sap was never flowing through them. Just make sure that they stay clean and fresh-looking.

There is a recent design fad of using artificial flowers that look like dried flowers. They have no energy. They never had sap flowing through them, and they look dead (dried). One of the reasons that making artificial flowers is such a noble craft is that it takes vibrant nature as its model. The dead version of a flower is not a desirable model. This is as true of artificial as it is of dried flowers.

Chapter 3:

Introduction to the Bagua

I was skeptical but intrigued when I first heard about the feng shui bagua. Skeptical, because it doesn't fit my worldview—I'm not ancient Chinese. But I was intrigued because it seemed as if you could play with it like a game. That's how I deal with it, and the results continue to amaze me.

It's one of feng shui's most powerful tools. The bagua (or pakua) is a grid with nine areas (or guas). See Fig. 14. The grid is a map that can be applied to divide a space into these nine areas, each of which corresponds to an aspect of life. The life aspect is influenced by the layout and contents of the corresponding part of the living space.

The bagua is the one part of Form School feng shui that doesn't immediately relate to common sense for most folks. That's because it's a construction based on the concept of yin/yang—balanced energy flow. A bagua map is just a great big yin/yang symbol flopped down over the floorplan of your home (or room). See Fig. 15. You step into the yin side (dark) and in front of you is the yang. Yang's official color is red (for fire) although it's often shown as white, because black and white are seen as visual opposites in the West. The most basic purpose of the bagua is to express *balance*.

Bagua map

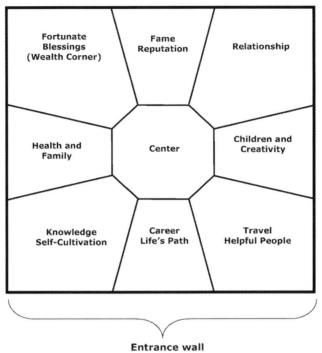

Entrance wall

Fig. 14

A refinement of the yin/yang concept is the Taoist teaching of the five elements (with their associated shapes, colors, and relationships to one another). The five elements do not refer to the strictly physical realm. They represent archetypal energies, and as they move from most yin to most yang, they are Water, Metal, Earth, Wood, and Fire. Earth is considered to be neutral, between yin and yang, and the three Earth areas of the bagua are in a diagonal line and separate the yin from the yang. Many books have been written about the elements and much of acupuncture is based on them. Each of the nine areas has an element that is associated with it. The areas and elements are:

Life's Path	—	Water
Knowledge	—	Earth
Health and Family	—	Wood
Fortunate Blessings	—	Wood
Fame	—	Fire
Relationship	—	Earth
Children and Creativity	—	Metal
Helpful People and Travel	—	Metal
Center	—	Earth

There are five areas that relate most strongly to their elements. The shape that represents the element is identified with each of these five areas. These are the five areas that are not in corners:

Life's Path (Water)	—	Freeform or wavy
Health and Family (Wood)	—	Vertical/Rectangular
Fame (Fire)	—	Angular (such as a pyramid or cone)
Children and Creativity (Metal)	—	Round, oval, or arched
Center (Earth)	—	Horizontal/Rectangular, or Square

All the areas have certain colors that relate to them. The five areas just listed have colors that are symbolized by their element. They are:

Life's Path (Water) — Black

Health and Family (Wood) — Green and Blue

Fame (Fire) — Red

Children and Creativity (Metal) — White or Pastels

Center (Earth) — Yellow, Brown, or any Earth tone

The other four areas, which are the corner guas, have colors that are arrived at by a meeting and blending of the colors in the two areas on each side. For example, the white of the Creativity area meets the red of the Fame area, making the pink of the Relationship area. Red and white are also appropriate in the Relationship area.

There are *I Ching* trigrams that relate to each of the bagua areas except the center. These eight trigrams are considered to be a useful Taoist tool for classifying the manifest energy of creation. The *I Ching* oracle consists of sixty-four hexagrams that are composed of all the possible combinations of the eight trigrams. The *I Ching* is a very ancient book and the translation that I recommend is *The Book of Changes and the Unchanging Truth*, reviewed in Recommended Reading.

Yin Yang Bagua over House

House Outline

Front Door

Illustration 15.

CHART OF BAGUA AREAS

Area (Gua)	Alternate Names	Element	Color	Shape
Life's Path	Career The Journey	Water	Black and very dark colors	Freeform
Knowledge	Contemplation Wisdom Meditation Intuition	Earth	Black, dark green, and dark blue	
Health and Family	Ancestors Elders Community New Beginning	Wood	Green and blue	Vertical, rectangular, or square
Fortunate Blessings	Wealth Empowerment Intention Abundance	Wood	Rich shades of purple, blue, and red Also green	
Fame	Reputation Illumination Future Recognition	Fire	Red, maroon, magenta, any shade of red, even including violet & purple	Angular, triangular, pointed, conical, or uprising
Relationship	Love Marriage Partnership Commitment	Earth	Pink, white, red, and yellow	
Children and Creativity	Descendants Completion Joy Pleasure	Metal	White and pastels	Circular, oval, or arched
Helpful People and Travel	Benefactors Compassion Determination Persistence	Metal	Black, white, or gray	
Center	Health Unity Tai Chi Wholeness	Earth	Yellow and earth tones such as brown, gold, and orange	Horizontal, square, rectangular or octagonal

I Ching trigram	Meaning of Trigram	Comments
	Water	Perfect place for a fountain, or picture of water flowing into the room.
	Mountain	Good place for books and learning tools, including television or computer or audio equipment.
	Thunder	Good place for plants and images of plants. Wooden furniture, especially tall.
	Wind	Expensive items, things that move or shimmer. No open trashcans. Great place for a fountain or picture of water. Also plants or pictures of plants are good here.
	Fire	Items related to fame such as awards. Things representing animals or made of animals—fur, bone, leather, feathers, etc. Also things made of plastic or that use electricity.
	Earth	Pictures of loved ones, pairs and groupings of things. No outstanding singular objects. No TV.
	Lake	Items that relate to children, and/ or creativity. If you have kids, the maintenance of this area will affect them.
	Heaven or Father	Images of deities, angels, holy people, teachers, or mentors. A good place for spiritual affirmations.
No trigram		No bathroom, ever! A good place for pottery. Keep this area open and traversable.

ELEMENTAL CYCLES

The five elements relate to each other in several powerful and dynamic cycles. Upon first reading, the elemental cycles can seem overwhelming in complexity, but they actually stay pretty close to common sense.

In the *creative (or helping) cycle* each element is considered to give birth to the next element.

Wood	creates	Fire	(Wood is the fuel)
Fire	creates	Earth	(Ashes are as dirt)
Earth	creates	Metal	(Through time and pressure)
Metal	creates	Water	(Through condensation)
Water	creates	Wood	(Water is essential to plants)

The *destructive (or controlling) cycle* is not the reverse of the creative cycle. The interaction is rearranged, and the second element is hindered.

Wood	destroys	Earth	(Plants eat dirt)
Earth	destroys	Water	(The result is mud)
Water	destroys	Fire	(Quite obviously)
Fire	destroys	Metal	(Through melting)
Metal	destroys	Wood	(Axes and saws kill trees)

There is also what is known as the *conflicting (or weakening) cycle* which is similar to the destructive cycle, but not usually as strong. It is the exact reverse of the creative cycle.

Wood	weakens	Water	(Eventually the water is consumed)
Water	weakens	Metal	(Rust)
Metal	weakens	Earth	(Metal is mined from the earth)
Earth	weakens	Fire	(Dirt smothers fire)
Fire	weakens	Wood	(Wood is consumed by fire)

Both the conflicting and destructive cycles can be called upon in deciding what to do when there is too much of an element in a dwelling (or room).

When there is too much:	Add:
Wood	Fire or Metal
Water	Fire, Earth, or Wood
Metal	Fire or Water
Earth	Wood, Water, or Metal
Fire	Earth or Water

There is a fourth cycle that is called the *mitigation cycle*. When two elements are in conflict, according to destructive cycle, there is an element that mitigates the conflict.

	Conflict		Mitigating Element
Water	with	Fire	Wood
Wood	with	Earth	Fire
Fire	with	Metal	Earth
Earth	with	Water	Metal
Metal	with	Wood	Water

Various teachers explain some of the details differently, such as why Metal creates Water. If you look at these cycles and their explanations only from the point of view of Western science and logic, you are missing the point. Remember to view the elements as an archetypal energy. They are a Taoist metaphor for how certain energy reacts when it meets other energies.

To see what represents any of the archetypal elements, refer to the Chart of Bagua Areas. Look up "Main Element," and then refer to its "Color," "Shape," and "Comments" sections.

For most people the first cycle, the creative cycle, is the easiest to work with. It lets you use green instead of red in the Fame area—wood feeds fire. So instead of using red towels (which tend to bleed) in a Fame bathroom, you could use green towels—any shade of green that you like. In a dark foyer that's located in the Life's Path area, you can use white and lots of it. White symbolizes Metal, which creates Water.

There is an aspect of landform that involves the elemental cycles. Your home, by its shape and construction materials, predominantly represents one of the five elements. The area around your home is also determined to represent one of the five elements. The interaction between the two elements is then evaluated. For instance, an asymmetrical home with lots of glass is Water. When the home sits amid round mountains, it is within a Metal environment, and that's good, because Metal generates Water. The outside environment produces the same element of which the home is made, thereby feeding its prosperity. This concept is tricky and usually requires contemplation. One of the most understandable explanations is in Angel Thompson's book, *Feng Shui* (see Recommended Reading). This knowledge is quite important for homeowners and those planning to buy a home. It's also useful to know when painting the outside of a house.

The information on elemental cycles is probably more complicated than anything else I've presented in *Feng Shui Demystified*. The following sums it up:

Water creates Wood, is created by Metal; weakens Fire, and is controlled by Earth.

Wood creates Fire, is created by Water; weakens Earth, and is controlled by Metal.

Fire creates Earth, is created by Wood; weakens Metal, and is controlled by Water.

Earth creates Metal, is created by Fire; weakens Water, and is controlled by Wood.

Metal creates Water, is created by Earth; weakens Wood, and is controlled by Fire.

Chapter 4:

The Bagua in Place

The bagua is used as a map to the life areas most associated with a particular part of a space. In arranging that space, you can consider that what you're seeing is a way to communicate with your higher self (or guide or guardian angel). The response back to you can seem as quick as e-mail or it can take up to a year. The average response occurs within a month. The way that you receive a response depends largely on your ability to notice "coincidences." That ability involves bright, open intuition and can be cultivated. When you realize that your higher self is "reading" what your living space looks like, your concept of your personal potential will, in some sense, begin to crumble. A more unlimited version will naturally take its place.

To use the bagua, imagine it enlarged and stretched to fit over your living space. An example of how a bagua is shaped for rectangular spaces is shown in Fig. 16.

The grid can be laid down over the floor plan of a room, apartment, or house. It can be applied to a space as large as a plot of land, or as small as a desktop. There are two very different ways to orient the bagua over a floor plan. One way is to use a compass, and place the Fame area toward the south. The other way is to use the main door as the orienting factor—this is the method I always use. The side of the bagua that has the Life's Path area is laid down along the wall that has the main entrance door. Both ways of using the bagua are valid, but trying to mix the two is not a good idea. My suggestion is that if you are already drawn to astrology or numerology, then give the compass method a try. Otherwise, try the kind of feng shui that uses the entrance to orient the bagua.

Bagua stretched to fit rectangular shape

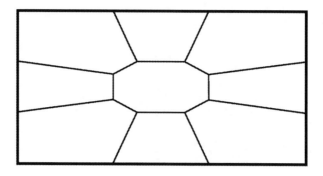

Fig. 16

Bagua Oriented by Compass Directions

This method draws heavily on Taoist numerology and astrology. Humanity has come up with many systems of thought to classify people. The enneagram is one such system, and Compass School feng shui is another system. In it, people are classified not only by their Chinese astrological sign (one of twelve animals) but also, and very importantly, by their element. Some practitioners also classify people by one of eight *I Ching* trigrams. All of these feng shui techniques are based on the person's birth time.

In using the compass method, the simple part is knowing how to orient the bagua—fame equals south—easy! Beyond that, things start to get complicated, because of the astrology and numerology involved. Once some basic calculations have been figured, you will know your element, your fortunate direction, and your fortunate number or star. The downside of that is that you will also find out that several directions are quite bad for you. Your spouse's lucky direction could easily be considered somewhat deadly for you. One of the questions that arises is which direction to orient the bed, so that it can be fortunate for one of the partners. In ancient China, it was an easy decision—make it good for the guy. (Remember, this was a culture that was so terrified by the power of the feminine that women's feet were kept bound until they were tiny stubs.) In the compass school, there aren't a lot of gray areas, things are either good for you or they're bad for you. The height of your table is either good for you, or it's bad for you—and, yes, there is a special ruler that is used to measure your furniture. On that ruler there are only two colors—one color signifying good for you, the other color meaning the size is bad for you—nothing in between. Your home gets divided into nine "magic" squares, and some of those squares are great for you, and others are thought to be quite terrible, with names like Death, Disaster, Bad Life, and Five Ghosts. Some people are put off by what they perceive as excess paranoia. Other folks relish the challenge, and appreciate how methodical and decisive it is.

Bagua Oriented by the Entrance

For those who choose to orient the bagua by the entrance, the task is as simple as lining up the main door (of an individual room or a whole house or apartment) along the side of the bagua that has the Life's Path area. When this is done correctly, the Fortunate Blessings area will always be to your far left when you have just entered a room. If there is ever a question as to which door to a room is the main door, it is usually the one close to the main front entrance. Any time the obvious main door has been blocked, and *absolutely cannot be used*, the secondary door should be used to orient the bagua. Also, if you walk into your home and immediately have to turn to continue into the home, the bagua is based on the direction of that turn. See Fig. 17.

Bagua based on turn

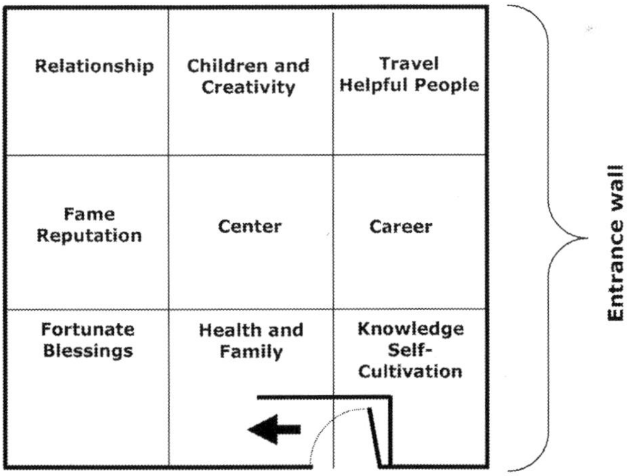

Relationship	Children and Creativity	Travel Helpful People
Fame Reputation	Center	Career
Fortunate Blessings	Health and Family	Knowledge Self-Cultivation

Entrance wall

Fig. 17

Every time you change floors in a house (even a few steps) you set up a new bagua. The direction you are facing when you first step onto a new level is how you orient the bagua, according to the entrance method. The only exception is if a wall is close in front of you, and causes you to immediately turn right or left. The bagua is then based on that turn. Also please realize that there are occasionally unique houses that require bending the rules. Well-cultivated intuition is the key.

What to do when you never (or almost never) use your front door? Many people always enter their homes through a side door from the carport or garage. If this door isn't on the same side of the building as the "formal front door," you've got two baguas for that house. One is based on the real front door and one is based on the side entrance. Neither can be totally discounted because both are important, but for different reasons. The formal front door is usually where packages are delivered and guests are received. The entrance you use all the time is important because you use it. Keep the side entrance looking nice, but it shouldn't compete with the formal front door, which should always be the most attention-getting. Maybe paint the outside of the side entrance door your very favorite color if it opens into a garage. That way you're giving yourself a big dose of something you love every time you come home.

This kind of feng shui accounts for much of its current popularity because Westerners can easily grasp the rationale behind it—basic energy movement. It is called various names, most commonly: intuitive, Black Sect, or eight-point. Since none of those names tells you much about it, for the sake of clarity I will refer to it as the entrance-based bagua. In a sense, it is an off-shoot of Form School feng shui, because it looks to the *form* of the house to find the "mouth" (the front door).

APPLYING THE BAGUA

When applying the bagua over places that overlap each other, such as a room within a house, the bagua for the individual room is most powerful. When you are in a room, that's the space that is affecting you the most at that time. Of all the rooms in a house, the bedroom is usually considered to be the most potent, because typically, people spend a third of their life there. The more time you spend in a room, the more effect it has on you. When applying the bagua per room, very small rooms such as bathrooms and foyers should almost always be looked at as part of the larger picture. They're a bit small to realistically lay down a bagua, and they're not places where people tend to "hang out."

The Chinese name for an individual area of the bagua is a *gua*. Divide the wall of the room (or house) in approximate thirds, and that will show you the location of the guas on that wall. The bagua may be drawn with pie-shaped guas or squareish guas, whichever you prefer. When drawn with squareish guas, the whole bagua resembles a tic tac toe drawing. See Fig.18. It also looks like the lo shu grid of Compass feng shui.

Bagua drawn with square shapes

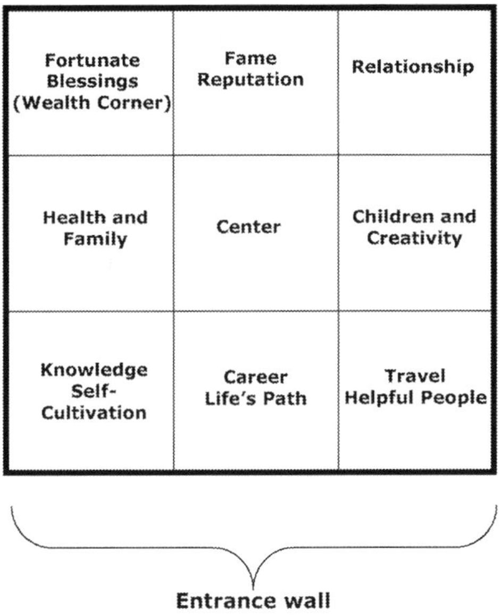

Fortunate Blessings (Wealth Corner)	Fame Reputation	Relationship
Health and Family	Center	Children and Creativity
Knowledge Self-Cultivation	Career Life's Path	Travel Helpful People

Entrance wall

Fig. 18

There is occasionally the situation where a door is at an angle to the rest of the room. The wall that is closest to the doorknob counts as the entrance wall. See Fig. 19. When an entire building has the front door at an angle and is located at an intersection, the street with the most traffic determines the entrance wall.

When a door to a room opens directly along a left or right wall, the chi is guided by that wall, builds up speed, and then knocks into the far corner ferociously. Some feng shui teachers maintain that when this happens, the area it hits is bounced along the wall to join the area at the other corner. This means that a Relationship area could be knocked into a Fortunate Blessings area, or vice-versa. It is not a bad situation; it's just something to be aware of. If there is an interruption along the wall, by a large piece of furniture, the bounce is only partial. In such a case, fifty percent of the Relationship area may be left in its original location and fifty percent may get bounced. If this happened, you would just want to be sure that the Fortunate Blessings area had some of the characteristics of the Relationship area—for example, pairs of objects.

Door in an angled wall

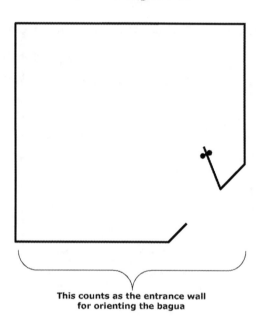

This counts as the entrance wall
for orienting the bagua

Fig. 19

When applying the bagua over an entire house with an attached garage, the question arises as to whether or not the garage should be included in the bagua. Disagreement abounds on this issue, and reputable teachers offer persuasive arguments pro and con. Some say always include the garage if the same roofline which defines the house also covers the garage. Others say that the garage is a place for parking cars, no one really lives there, so no need to include it in the bagua of the whole house. In my own practice, I do not usually include the garage unless it has been converted into a room, and is no longer a "home for cars."

Closets can have clothes hangers that are the appropriate color for their bagua location in the home. This is a cheap, easy way to enhance an area without disturbing a more visible color scheme. For instance, if the closet is in the Fame area, use red hangers.

INDIVIDUAL BAGUA AREAS

Here are the bagua areas, going clockwise around a room (or house).

Fortunate Blessings

This is the far left corner and it is always a great place to start. The *I Ching* trigram for this area is Wind, representing the winds of change. Another name for this area is Intention. Making improvements in this area is like waving a flag to the Universe. "Hey, I'm here!" It is most commonly referred to as the Wealth Corner, but it is important to remember that fortunate blessings can come to you in a lot more ways than just money. The Fortunate Blessings area provides a wonderful opportunity to prove the efficacy of feng shui for yourself. It is a very powerful area.

One of the basic things to know about this area is that *it must be clean, uncluttered, and well maintained.* If anything in this area is broken, either fix it or move it. Don't have furniture here that is intentionally distressed-looking—no "shabby chic." It is great to have plants here (the bigger the better) but they must be healthy, look vibrant, and have no thorns. Two plants that I frequently recommend for this area are Dieffenbachia (Dumb Cane) and Rhapis excelsa (Lady Palm). They are both quite easy to grow, not needing direct sun. The variegation and coloration of the Dieffenbachia leaves is quite reminiscent of dollar bills. The Rhapis is not cheap, but oh-so-elegant, especially with an uplight arising behind it.

As you might imagine, the "Wealth" area is an ideal place to put expensive things—things that were a stretch for you to afford. Paying more than you had planned for an object in the Fortunate Blessings area gives you what I call "the ouch factor." The symbolism comes alive in your life. It is much more real than something like a framed picture of an expensive car. Don't keep small change in this area or fake money. If you keep any actual money here, it should be real hundred dollar bills. Expensive things vary depending on the use of the room. In a kitchen, it would be fine to have a refrigerator in this area. In a living room or den, a television generally counts as a rather expensive object. Be aware that if the television or computer is in the Fortunate Blessings area, you *still* need to be able to see the door from your seated position. Use a mirror if necessary.

One of my clients was trying to sell a nice, but empty, house. (Empty houses are always harder to sell than those with just the right amount of furniture.) He was having no luck at all and I suggested that he pull up the very corner of the carpet in the Wealth Corner of the house and hide something expensive there, but that he could retrieve it once the sale was finalized. He said, "I have a ruby. Would that do?" I said, "If you're willing to put a ruby there, you'll probably be very pleased with the results." He did so and solid offers started coming in immediately, and the place sold quickly.

Color is a powerful tool in all areas of the bagua, and especially so in this area. Royal purple is ideal, as well as cobalt blue, and bold Chinese red. Green can also be a good color here, because wood is the element that is associated with this area. You want rich, vibrant, saturated colors, but you don't necessarily have to get out the paintbrush. If the colors are appropriately brilliant, you don't always have to use a lot to be effective. On the other hand, don't be afraid of overdoing it. If you like the idea of saturated purple walls in your Fortunate Blessings area, feng shui applauds you. Don't, however, change wall colors at an inward corner (a corner that juts into the room)—it will have a jarring effect in the room. Change wall colors only at an outward corner (a corner that goes back away from the center of the room). This is true especially if your home has bullnose (rounded) corners. See Fig. 20. I've seen homes where the wall color changes in the middle of a curving bullnose—the effect is like apologizing for having good architecture! The only time it's alright to change color at an inward corner is when vertical molding (usually white) has been added to that corner.

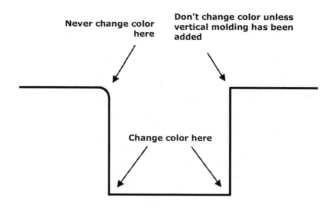

Changing paint colors within a room

Fig. 20

Fountains or aquariums are absolutely perfect in this area, since water represents money, but be sure to keep them running. A woman who attended one of my classes later told me this story. She and her husband own a coffee shop and had a certain goal of how much money they'd like to make in a day. They had come close but never achieved it, so she thought she'd put a fountain in the Wealth Corner of their home. The husband laughed at the idea, but she went ahead and within a week they achieved their goal and the next day they did even better. She decided to have some fun with him, so she said, "I think you're right about that fountain idea— I'm going to remove it." His response was, "Oh, no you don't!" He's not the first spouse to become a believer by seeing the results.

Windchimes are excellent here, since the *I Ching* trigram for this area is Wind. Garbage cans are not a good idea here, but if you must have one, it should have a lid. In the feng shui view of things, a garbage can here means you are throwing your wealth away, but a lid on it changes that dynamic. If your garbage can is in a cabinet (as they sometimes are in kitchens) it does not have to have a lid on it. Be especially aware of the symbolism of any pictures that are in the Fortunate Blessings area. Another name for this area is Empowerment. If you have pictures of people, ask yourself if you really want those people to be exercising influence in your life.

If the windows in the Fortunate Blessings area seem overly large, you might need to hang sheer curtains to keep the chi inside. (I never recommend brightly-colored sheer curtains anywhere, because they tint the light coming into the room.) If you choose lace, use the best you can afford for this area. Instead of sheers, you could hang a clear octagon crystal (or small windchime) in the window to symbolically disperse energy before it vanishes outside. This gua is generally not a good place for mirrors because they represent windows.

Fame

This area is related to the future, your reputation, and what people are saying about you. Fire is the element here, and it is the meaning of the *I Ching* trigram. It is represented by red—ideally a very brilliant primary red such as is used on stop signs and fire engines. Such a saturated color is not always appropriate to add to every interior situation. If, however, you need fame in your work, I advise you to learn to love this color. Thousands of dollars of publicity will not buy what the bold use of candy-apple red will achieve if used in the Fame area. If you need fame, you cannot overdo it. For those people who just want a good reputation, tone it down. Maroon, old rose, magenta, or violet—even purple—basically any color that is in the warm end of the spectrum will have a good effect. Earth-tone reds are the only reds that aren't good in this area. Colors such as terra cotta, orange, and yellow represent Earth and if you throw earth on a fire, the fire goes out.

When I put red curtains in my own Fame area, within a month a major television station called to feature me in their *Evening Magazine*. A client who is an artist painted the laundry room of his studio red, because it was in his Fame area. Within a week he called at seven in the morning asking if I had seen the newspaper—"I'm on the cover in color!"

The shape of Fire is pointed, like a flame going up. Cones, pyramids, triangles, or any shape that is sharply angular is appropriate. A few examples of this are red triangular cushions on a couch, red tapered candles, or a picture of buildings with red, pointed roofs. Fireplaces are auspicious in this area, if they are used a lot. A fireplace without a fire burning just represents the material of which it is made, Earth or Metal.

A mirror in the Fame area is useful to help move you into the future, because one of the names for this area is Future. It's even better if the mirror has a sunburst frame.

The Fame area is the one place where I most definitely do *not* recommend water features (such as fountains) or representations of water (such as ocean pictures). It is somewhat unfortunate to have a bathroom in the Fame area, because of the amount of water involved. If this is the case in your home, you'll need to add as much red as you can stand—red rugs, red towels, red shower curtain, red soap squirter, and so forth. (Be aware that red towels tend to "run" if laundered with other colors.) Candles are great here—even if they aren't burning, their material still represents Fire.

This area is perfect for hanging diplomas or awards, especially with red frames or red matting. This is one of the few areas where I would recommend the plant Sansevieria (Snake Plant or Mother-in-law's-tongue). It has a flame-like form that almost no other plant can match. It will also grow in almost complete darkness, and is as pest-free as they come for indoor plants. If you just must have thorny houseplants, this is the one and only area where I can say okay to them.

Animals are considered to have "the fire of life" within them, so items of animal origin are appropriate here. Such things might be made of leather, feathers, bone, horn, or fur. Pictures or figurines of animals are also good. I would avoid things that come from or represent sea animals in this area, such as seashells or sand dollars or pictures of fish or sea mammals. I put a drum which had leather on top in my Fame area and within a week, *The San Francisco Chronicle* called asking if I wanted to be on the cover of the Sunday edition business section. I said yes.

Plastic represents Fire as do any items that use electricity.

Relationship

This is the far right corner and the *I Ching* trigram for this area is Earth. The area is associated with all relationships, not just romantic partnerships. The most important thing to note about this area is that there should be no outstanding singular objects here. If there is a torchière, it should be supported by more than one pole, or have more than one bulb. It is best if things in this area relate to each other. There is a design concept that things are either in conflict or in conversation. In this area, they need to be in conversation. For pictures, it would be best if they were in pairs or groupings. If there is only one picture, it should have several items within it, such as a group of flowers, or a couple of people.

One of my clients had pictures of single women all over her house, including in her Relationship area. She, herself, was single but didn't want to be. I had warned her about the "message" that she was sending out to the Universe by having all the single women pictures, but she loved them too much to part with them. Finally I said, "What would you rather have—these pictures or a real person to cuddle with?" She said, "You've just said it in a way that reached me." And she immediately went to her Relationship corner and took away a big picture of a single woman. That weekend she met a man who literally swept her off her feet and gave her what she described as "the kiss of a lifetime." There's a lot of power in doing something immediately and not procrastinating.

This is an ideal place to put collections of things, as well as books, especially with matching bookends. Anything that might represent conflict, such as guns or swords, should never be kept in the Relationship area. Don't keep kitchen knives visible within this area. Avoid fabric with stripes on it (considered to represent conflict) in this area.

A friend of mine had been in a committed relationship for many years, and while walking through her yard one day I noticed that she had started keeping broken pottery (for mosaic projects) in the Relationship area. I strongly cautioned her about it, but she kept it there and within a few months her relationship ended and she was heartbroken. Don't have *anything* broken in this area, and to be on the safe side, I wouldn't even have mosaics made of broken pottery here.

Pink is the color of love and is the ideal color for this area—any shade of pink, including dusty rose, which is much easier to live with than most pinks. Most pinks, especially bright pinks, aren't good for men. In fact they're best used in large doses only for young girls (who might want them.) Red, white, and yellow also work in this area. Remember the color doesn't *have* to be the dominant color; it just needs to be there someplace.

Things that have a romantic association are appropriate here. Televisions are not so appropriate because they can signify a life in which that object is the main relationship. If there is no other place to have the television, it is best to cover it when it is not in use. It is also good to have something above the television, such as pictures on the wall. Telephones or computers are fine in the Relationship area, because we use them both to communicate. Do not ever have thorny or spiky plants here. A heart shape can symbolize love, but a single heart can say "lonely heart," so if you have any, have at least two hearts.

Before I met the partner of my life, I was living in a studio apartment built around the 1930's. The Relationship area was a small, all-white bathroom with a very tall ceiling. My method of bringing a "romantic" look to this space was to hang a large basket fairly high on the one wall that had room for it. I filled the basket with pink silk lotus flowers—lots of them! When they arrived in the mail, they were quite crushed and I got on a chair and took a very long time carefully arranging them so that each petal and leaf looked completely natural. When I stepped off the chair, I liked what I saw. I put my arms akimbo and said, "Boy, your phone is gonna *ring*." Two seconds later my phone rang with someone asking for a date! Six months later I met my soulmate.

The *I Ching* trigram for the Relationship area is all yin lines so this area especially affects women and feminine energy.

Children and Creativity

If you don't have kids, this area is about your ideas and creativity, because they are basically what you leave behind when you pass away. If you do have kids, this area will always affect them, even if they are not living with you. It will also affect their offspring. If this area becomes overly cluttered, or ill-maintained, you can expect such things as bad grades on report cards. It is a great place to put pictures or mementos of your children. The *I Ching* trigram for this area is the Lake.

Metal is the element here, and is represented by white or any pastel tones. The glint of sunlight on silver is considered to be white. Objects that have a metallic finish are also appropriate. The shape for Metal is round (because coins are universally round and metal), with oval or arched being equally good. Creativity is associated with this element, and the rounded shapes help ideas *flow*. Some objects that are very appropriate here are very creative artwork, round mirrors, decorative round metal wall plates, pots and pans (if it's a kitchen), and lamps or pole lights that are metal and have round shapes. In general, round lamps are preferred anywhere in the home because round symbolizes completion—full circle.

Helpful People and Travel

You may or may not want to travel, but everyone needs helpful people in life. Both of these unrelated aspects are addressed in this gua. If you are hoping to travel, or if you just want to make sure that you will have help when you need it, keep this area nice—clean and uncluttered. Pictures of far-away places are great to put in this area, as well as objects that came from far away. It's also a good place for images of people that you think of as your mentors, teachers, or benefactors. People who help you can be thought of as "heaven sent." Heaven is the *I Ching* trigram for this area. Images of deities or holy people would be appropriate here, as well as images of angels or guardian beings. Any items that have come from other lands would be helpful here.

This is an area for neutral tones—white, black, or gray. The element that is associated with this area is Metal, so metal or round objects are quite appropriate here.

This area especially affects men, and masculine energy. If you have images of angels or deities here, they should not look feminine. If this area is missing (or is a garage) don't be surprised if there is no man in that home. In the home of one single woman there was a small bookshelf in this area, and as I looked over her books I suggested that she put the books by male authors there.

Life's Path

This area is sometimes referred to as the Career area, but it represents a lot more than just what you do to earn money. It has to do with your journey through life. The *I Ching* trigram for this area is Water. One of the most powerful things you can do in the use of feng shui is to put a representation of flowing water in the Life's Path area. Since Water is the element associated with this area, waterfall pictures are great here. Pictures of ponds or lakes are not ideal, because the water is basically stagnant. For the same reason, ocean pictures are out, because the water is mostly sloshing around. It is best to use pictures of rivers or streams. In this case, the water is going somewhere just by following a natural law—gravity. By representing this in the Life's Path area, you are setting up a dynamic in your own life to keep yourself on track with your life's purpose. No smacking your forehead and saying, "What was *that* year all about?" Water features such as fountains and aquariums are absolutely ideal in this area.

I knew someone who put a fountain in her Career area and got fired the same day. Naturally I asked for more details. She said, "The fountain had a light beneath the water." (That symbolizes conflict, because "fire" is under water, which is not usually a natural occurrence, and when it does happen in nature, it's an explosive situation.) She also said, "It was one of those fountains with a little stone ball that rolls around as the water emerges, but that part never worked." She had installed two messages in her Career area: "conflict" and "not working." She had used water as the medium for the messages, and Water is the element in that area. Her message got an instant reply. Remember, it's wise to consider the *details* of what you are doing in feng shui.

Black or dark blue are the ideal colors in this area, but if that just isn't you, go for whatever dark tones appeal to you. Even dark furniture will do. Black represents water because it is as if you are looking into a deep, dark well. The shape for water is freeform, like a river meandering or drop that splashed. Items made of glass are great to use here, especially if they have a watery feel, such as glass blocks. Mirrors also represent water. If you have furniture like a 50's kidney-shaped coffee table, this is definitely a great place for it. If there are drapes, let them be long and "puddle" on the floor.

If you are undergoing a career change, be sure this area stays clutter-free to allow fresh energy to flow in easily. Items that have to do with your career, such as diplomas, are appropriate in this area—perhaps in a black frame and black matting.

Knowledge and Self-Cultivation

Wisdom, Meditation, and Contemplation are other names for this area, and it is an excellent place for an altar. The *I Ching* trigram is Mountain, and it is a great place to put pictures of mountains. Likewise, it is a good place for images of deities, spiritual teachers, and wise people. It would be best to leave out images of water unless they are on the entrance wall close to the door. This is because the element Earth is associated with this area, and the mixing of Earth and Water creates mud. Black, blue, and green are the ideal colors, but the blue and green should be dark, navy tones. Books and other learning tools are appropriate here, including televisions, computers, and stereos. When a television is in this area, you probably have the extra advantage of being empowered because you won't have to turn your head to see the entrance. Items made of pottery are good because clay is Earth.

Health and Family

The family that this area is referring to is your ancestors—your parents and those who came before them. Put pictures of those people here. They are able to offer more resonance in your life from this gua. That this area also represents health is appropriate since our genes can predispose us to certain health conditions or immunities.

The *I Ching* trigram here is Thunder, and the best colors are any shades of green and/or blue. Sage green is one of the most livable colors for interior walls.

Because Wood is the element, plants are perfect in the Health/Family area, especially trees such as ficus or palms. Representations of plants are also good—any pictures of healthy growing plants, especially trees. Wooden objects are ideal here. Metal objects are not so ideal, metal implements being a major destroyer of living trees. Fireplaces are also not a good idea in this area. They are dealt with in Chapter 6.

The shape for Wood is vertical rectangular, like tall growing trees. Square is also good. Tall wooden furniture such as shelves, cabinets, or armoires, is perfect to use in this area.

Center

Just as the earth joins all things on this planet into a dynamic interdependence, the center of the bagua joins all the perimeter guas together. Its element is Earth, and in ancient China (and many other cultures) the center of a house was often an open-to-the-air courtyard. Here one walked across actual earth to reach the various areas of the house. The healthiest living spaces I have seen are those in which the center (of the room, house, or apartment) is open and uncluttered. It is very important for human traffic to be able to flow through this area. I once had a neighbor who lived in a small studio apartment. His bed was a folding futon, but he never folded it into a couch, preferring to keep it out as a bed at all times. The center of his apartment was *deliberately* blocked and untraversable, and it showed in his life. He was constantly frustrated, floundering, and slowly getting nowhere in his life. One of the key factors here was that he had the *choice* of unblocking his center area, but didn't. If people create their own problems, the consequences can be more severe, especially when they know better.

This area concerns your health, and your ability to integrate all of who you are into a healthy personality. Earth is represented by yellow or any earth tones such as ochre or brown. The shape is square or rectangular. Pottery, stones, natural crystals, and beautiful sand are all ways to bring real earth into this area. Fireplaces and stairs, especially spiral stairs, are not good in the Center. Also fountains and other water features are not recommended in the Center because the element is Earth, and when Water and Earth are together, the result is mud. This is also the reason that there is a caution about water in the Knowledge area. There is no *I Ching* trigram for the center.

BATHROOM LOCATION

The location of the bathroom, more than that of any other room, can make or break a house. The most important thing is this: Don't have a bathroom in the center! This means that you shouldn't have a bathroom that is enclosed within a house. It must touch an outside wall. See Fig. 21. If you live in an apartment, the outside wall can just be the perimeter of your apartment. If you can walk in rooms of your house all around the bathroom, it counts as being in the center. Do not ever buy a house like this! Throughout the history of humanity, toilets have usually been outbuildings. It is only comparatively recently that they are located under the same roof as the living space. To bring them into the *core* of that space just doesn't work energetically! I have known the histories of some of those buildings—bankruptcy, divorce, disease, and so forth.

A healthy bathroom

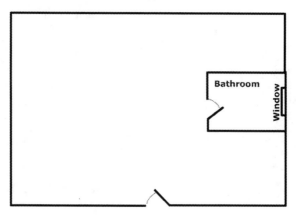

At least one side is tangent to an outside wall, preferably
with a window.

Fig. 21

A few years before I started learning feng shui, my partner and I moved into home with a bathroom in the very center. The people who were living in the place when we first saw it were living like human pigs, and the husband was in one bedroom and the wife and her boyfriend were living in the other bedroom. They were defaulting on their loan and the owner was out-of-state. When we spoke to the owner, we found out that the reason he sold the house in the first place was that he went broke and had to move away. After we moved into the home, our relationship lasted only six more months. I found out later that the home sold at a loss.

Another time I received a phone call from a desperate-sounding woman. She began enumerating her problems, such as her daughter's recurring kidney infection that was causing her to miss a lot of school. The latest thing that had happen was a car bomb! I just stopped her and said, "Where's your bathroom?" She said it was in the very center of the home. I carefully explained the problem and I guess I had enough veracity in my voice because she said, "I'll call you again when we've moved."

If you already live in a home with a totally enclosed toilet, I urge you to relocate the bathroom, or move. If that is impossible, here's a list of some things you can do to *partially help* the situation. They are listed in order from the most effective to the least effective. It would be ideal to do them all:

- If there is more than one bathroom in the house, do not use the center one. Guests may use it. If there is a skylight, grow lots of plants so that it seems like a greenhouse.
- Mirror all the walls (including the ceiling) of the bathroom one hundred percent. I know that sounds pretty weird, but feng shui doesn't consider this to be a mild situation. A more acceptable alternative is to cover all the walls in the bathroom with reflective material such as wallpaper (shiny side facing the bathroom), then paint or re-wallpaper right over it. The reflective side is acting as a sealing agent, keeping the drain vibes in that one room. Covering the material will not affect its sealing ability. Silver-leaf wallpaper is available—see Sources.
- Keep the door closed (as with any bathroom), and preferably mirrored on the outside.
- Put a bagua mirror on the outside of the bathroom above the door.

It is also not good to have a bathroom in the Fortunate Blessings area of the house or apartment. In this case, however, there *is* a lot you can do to change the dynamic:

- The toilet lid should always be down when not in use. It is actually important to have the lid already down when you push the handle to flush.
- The door should always be closed, and preferably mirrored on the outside. Hardware stores sell hinge-pin closers for a few dollars. They are easy to install, and will automatically shut the door.

- Put one or two large rounded stones at the rear base of your toilet. Glue felt to their bottoms if there's any chance of damage to floor tiles. The stones act as a grounding medium. They're large. They're solid. They couldn't possibly get flushed. They're gonna stay there!
- The plant Sansevieria (Snake Plant) can be used effectively around the toilet to counter the "flush" vibration. Its strong uprising form very effectively says "no" to that down-and-out vibration. Place it in pots on the floor on each side of the toilet tank. Snug the pots right up against the wall, and as far under the tank as they can go without bending the leaves. If your tank is out from the wall a bit, you might even have leaves coming up from behind the tank. Of course don't have any of the leaves terribly close to the seat.
- Affix a small mirror to the bathroom ceiling directly over the toilet seat, reflecting down onto the toilet. Double-sided foam tape works well.
- The trashcan should be hidden from view. Either put it in a cabinet, or use a trashcan with a lid.
- Make that bathroom the finest room in your house—fit for royalty. Spare no expense. Make it nice. It should be ultra-clean, and not cluttered.
- The accessories should be purple, blue, green, or red—rich, beautiful tones, not pastels.
- A very small windchime should be hung from the ceiling so that when the door to the bathroom has opened just a few inches it lightly touches the windchime making a very gentle sound.

If these nine guidelines are strictly adhered to, you will have dramatically changed the situation. It will have gone from a financial "drain" to something similar to a perpetual motion money machine. My best friend in San Francisco, Lilli, had a bathroom in her Wealth Corner and for three years I told her what to do. She always hemmed and hawed and said, "I never have enough money." Finally she followed my advice to the letter and made that room *royal* and within one month she was on the phone to me with these exact words, "I don't know what to do with all this money!" Shortly thereafter she took a month-long trip to Australia and the *entire* trip cost her $50. She was able to buy her own home in the Bay Area—something I didn't think she'd ever be able to do.

It is also a good idea not to have a bathroom visible from the front door. If that is the case in your home, be very sure to keep the bathroom door closed! When a bathroom door is closed, it's just *a door*—it could be a door to a closet or anything else—it doesn't cause the mind to think "bathroom." Place a mirror either on or above the outside of the bathroom door to symbolically push energy away from that room. If that door is not kept closed, it is thought to portend kidney or bladder problems.

It is best if the bathroom door is not oriented in the same direction as the front door of the home. When it *is* oriented in the same direction, put a small mirror outside the bathroom, on the wall opposite the bathroom door, facing the bathroom door. The little mirror is showing the door and is symbolically moving it to a different wall.

When you store a plunger next to the toilet, the message is, "This toilet is frequently dysfunctional." If that is really the case, then by all means repair the toilet and store the plunger out of sight.

Chapter 5:

Extensions and Missing Areas

One other very important aspect of working with the bagua is to make sure the entire square or rectangle of your house actually is all there. A perfect square or rectangle is considered to be the ideal shape for a floor plan. Any deviation from that should be thought of as either an extension or a missing area. Extensions (such as bay windows) are generally to your benefit, but missing areas can be a big problem.

Sometimes it is as obvious as day and night if a dwelling has an extension or missing area, but often it is a bit trickier than that. Different feng shui teachers use slightly different formulas to decide.

A common method is to consider whether the part of the building (or room) that extends is less than 50% of the total area in question. The "total area in question" is shown in gray on the illustrations in this chapter. If the building part is less than 50% of the total area in question, you've got an extension. Fig. 22 shows an extension. Figures 23 and 24 show missing areas. In these cases the building part is more than 50% of the total area in question.

Extension

Fig. 22

Point **A**

Missing Area

Fig. 23

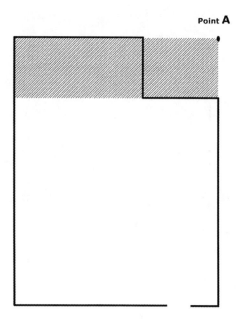

Point **A**

Missing Area

Fig. 24

BRINGING BACK A MISSING AREA

A mirror (the larger the better) placed on an inside wall of the missing area, facing the living space, is an effective solution. The mirror works symbolically with an "Alice through the looking glass" effect. It represents a door or window into another interior space, as it were. Also try to inhabit the missing area to whatever degree is possible, by adding such things as windowboxes, birdfeeders, or windchimes placed outside. Basically try to claim the area in a way that is appropriate.

If you have a patio or porch in the missing area, place chairs there (and a table if there is enough room). Don't use it as a haphazard or catchall storage area.

If windchimes are used outside a window in a missing area, the result can vary depending on how *appropriate* a windchime is, soundwise, for everyone who actually hears it. Do all members of a household like the sound? Do not impose loud, clanking sounds on your neighbors. Be sensitive to the proximity of neighbors' bedrooms. Disturbing your neighbors is not good sense, and it is not good feng shui.

Small wind-catchers are silent. Some of the windcatchers with colorful threads are so small that they can be used in almost any situation. You should see these as yet another opportunity to bring the correct shape and/or color into the missing area.

Lighting the missing area is very helpful. Strands of tiny clear holiday lights are often appropriate, and easy to use. They are also excellent for giving spatial definition (i.e., you can outline your space). Any light is better than none.

Do not let your imagination stagnate when it comes to inhabiting a missing area.

Note where point A is in both Figures 11 and 12. It is the apex of whichever area is missing. Try to keep that apex (point A) quite accessible. If possible, do something attention-getting at that point. Frequently used items are:

- An outdoor pole lamp
- A fountain
- A birdbath or birdfeeder
- A clothesline

By placing something very noticeable at the apex, you are giving that missing area some much-needed spatial definition.

I had a client with a missing Relationship area and one of her main goals for the consultation was to "get a man." The garage was behind the house and the driveway curved so that the apex of the missing Relationship area was in the driveway. I suggested that she glue two coins together face-to-face and then glue them to the cement. She started smiling and said, "I have a foreign coin collection and I'm going to have great fun going through them to pick the appropriate coins." I saw her at a booksigning several months later and she came up to me and said, " I want you to know I'm meeting the highest-quality men I've ever met in my life, and get this—they're all foreign!"

If the apex of a missing area is in the bottom of a swimming pool, use waterproof glue to affix one or more coins there.

WINDOWBOXES

If a missing area is above the first floor there's a window opening onto the missing area, that window is often your greatest friend for "claiming" some of that outside area. Using windowboxes is almost always my number one choice, for several reasons:

- You have agreed to a fairly frequent revisiting of that space, because if there are real, growing plants in the windowboxes, they are going to have to be watered. You need to realize that windowboxes benefit greatly from frequent watering. *Make sure the drainage is good*, and that no plants are left sitting in water.
- They are not difficult to install if the exterior walls are wood. Hardware stores sell special brackets made just for windowboxes. If you move, just fill in the holes made by the screws. Exterior masonry walls are more difficult, requiring masonry molly bolts.
- Windowboxes connect you to the earth. Even if you choose to use artificial flowers in the windowboxes, you are *still* more connected to the earth than if you weren't using windowboxes at all. If you are growing plants in your windowboxes, you are reestablishing some of the earth's biosystem where it was displaced or erased by the construction of your dwelling.

If you are a gardener (or are willing to learn) you can transform a lowly windowbox into a glorious celebration of plant life. Use the plant colors to enhance whichever area of the bagua is missing. If you are a true gardening beginner, I recommend some easy plants to get started with:

- Nasturtiums (leaves, flowers, and immature seedpods are all edible).
- Marigolds (edible flowers)
- Variegated Mediterranean herbs such as sage, thyme, and oregano
- Miniature variegated ivy
- Any succulent with rounded leaves, such as a jade plant or sedum. Check local nurseries to see which succulents grow well in your area.

Windowboxes can be an appropriate beginning place for a larger bio-reclaiming. If you can put a birdfeeder out the window, please do so. The windowbox can act to catch any birdseed that is spilled (if the spilled birdseed could bother any downstairs neighbors). If a birdfeeder with seed just won't work in your situation, in the Americas you can use an inexpensive hummingbird feeder that securely suctions onto the outside of your window.

Windowboxes are a natural place to put stones and crystals. The shape and color of the stone (or crystal) can be used to enhance whichever area of the bagua is missing. A rose quartz obelisk would be ideal in the Fame area. An amethyst crystal in a ball shape or in its natural form would be ideal in the Fortunate Blessing area. "Pairs of things" is the principle to always remember in the Relationship area. Figurines and statues are great to use in a windowbox in this area, always in groups or pairs.

Windowboxes are advantageous in many situations:

- To hide a bad view. No matter how wretched the view might have been, window boxes can change it to birds, butterflies, and flowers.
- To distract from a view that is commanding too much chi. This is any view that grabs you the instant you walk into a room.
- To bring back a missing area.

Chapter 6:

Architectural Features

Doors

If the knob of any door can touch the knob of any other door, you have a situation known as "clashing knobs." The knobs symbolize heads butting against each other, and most likely there will be arguments in that room or house. Sometimes it is possible to simply hang one of the doors on the opposite side of the doorframe. If that can't be done, then tie red ribbons or tassels from each knob that can touch another one. If you live alone, you might assume that there is usually no one around to argue with, so why bother? Well, you can always argue with yourself, and that means having a difficult time making up your mind. I know the red ribbons can look awkward, but the right tassels can look splendid.

When a door is close to a side wall, it is preferable that the hinges be on the side of the doorframe closest to the side wall. This insures that when the door is opened, the first thing that comes into view is the openness of the room. Otherwise, the first view would be of a wall, and the effect somewhat stifling. If this is the case, and you can't rehang the door from the other side, put a picture that shows perspective on the wall that you first see. You could put a mirror there instead, or you could put a mirror *behind* the picture. See Fig. 25. That way when the door opens, at least there's a *view* of openness.

Just as doors to rooms can cause poison arrows when left ajar, doors to cabinets can do the same. Be sure to close them.

Door opening to wall with correction

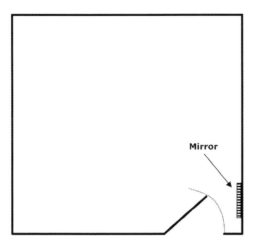

Fig. 25

Three doors in a row

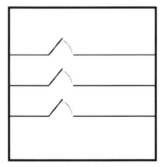

Fig. 26

Three doors in an *exact* row (Fig. 26) are a major feng shui problem, especially when all three doors are interior doors. They confuse chi energy in a unique way causing it not to disperse in the rooms properly. The problem is a *bit* less if one of the doors is external. Not two of the doors, *one* of the doors, as in

Fig. 27. If two of the three doors are external it's a severe problem. Energy won't tend to stay in the home well unless one of the doors is moved. (Note: this is not the same as three doors side-by-side (Fig. 28) which is usually quite harmonious.) The only real remedy is to move one of the doors, as in Fig. 29. That's usually not feasible, so the standard symbolic remedy is to hang one or more crystals anywhere above the pathway through the three doors. A very tall piece of furniture, such as a screen or bookshelf, could also be placed in one of rooms so that all three doorways aren't visible at once. Be careful not to make the space feel awkward if you do that.

Three doors in a row

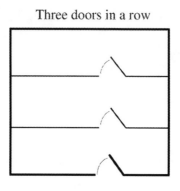

One of the doors is an external door

Fig. 27

Three doors side by side

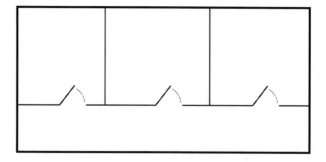

Illustration 28

One of the doors is moved

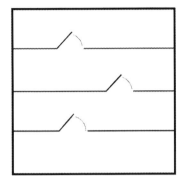

The three doors are no longer in a direct line

Illustration 29

WINDOWS

Another architectural feature that causes arguments is square windows. They have become quite popular in postmodern architecture, but they are a horrible idea according to feng shui. If you've got them, you probably can't do anything about them, but I would advise putting up drapes, shades, or blinds in such a way that the windows *seem* more rectangular. If you happen to have any round or arched windows, they give your house more Metal energy, and aid in creativity.

The ideal window in feng shui is one that opens fully (such as a casement window), not one that can only open halfway at a time (such as a double-hung window). Windows, like doors, allow chi to enter your life. Windows that open fully allow you to reach your potential more easily. The vitality of fresh air *is* chi energy. Let it into your home. Do not let your windows be stuck. Besides all the great fresh chi, just the act of opening and closing windows brings activity into the apex of a gua. The apex is important because it is where your realm extends farthest into the world.

Windows also represent your "inner eyes," your ability to see and know what you should be doing in your life. Clean windows allow you to do that fully. One of my clients had huge double-hung windows, but they were stuck, and they were filthy. She got a handyperson to unstick them, and I showed her the easy way to clean them using a squeegee (see *Spring Cleaning* in Recommended Reading). A few weeks later, I got a call from her saying she was going to move. I said, "What? You just went to all that trouble!" She replied, "I have a house north of the city that I've just been renting out because I didn't know what to do with it. Now I know that I should be living there. It seems obvious now, and I feel very solid about the decision." Hats off to clean windows!

Another thing that windows can represent is children (if you have children). The doors in the house would represent adults (i.e., parents). If the total ratio of windows to all doors is more than three-to-one, you could possibly have a problem with discipline. In other words, the children might rule.

POLES

A structural free-standing column is sometimes just called a pole. From a design point of view, central poles are often an awkward architectural feature. From a feng shui point of view, they represent split vision—people (or just yourself) not agreeing on what to do. Poles are usually load-bearing, so removing them is often out of the question. One suggestion would be to symbolically join them to a nearby wall. This can be done by putting screens or tall furniture (such as shelving) between the pole and the nearest wall. You now effectively have a room divider. And if that won't work in your situation, my second suggestion is to put a tall plant right next to the pole, somewhat hiding it. A split-leaf philodendron might be ideal, because it could use the pole for support. Otherwise, any tall plant would work fine. If the central pole is very large it is often recommended to put custom-cut mirrors on all sides of it, covering it completely. Do not use mirror tiles.

If none of the above solutions will work in your situation, put a very small mirror on the pole (shiny side facing away from the pole) and say out loud that you are thereby erasing the pole. If it's an extremely minimalist situation, where even a tiny mirror would be noticed, you could put one piece of silver glitter on the pole at the very bottom or at the very top. Just be sure to say out loud why you are doing it (to symbolize erasing the pole). It's the best you can do in the situation. At least you're doing *something* and that's good enough.

Poles that are near the edge of a room (or porch) are not a problem at all. They simply help define the space.

FIREPLACES

Fireplaces can let chi energy flow into them, and then up and out of your home. When not in use, it is preferable that they have good solid screening over them. There are three areas where a fireplace can be especially troublesome:

- Directly opposite the front door, and easily visible from that door. Chi flies straight into it, then up and out the chimney.
- The Center of the house (or room) is a problem because it represents the core and that energy *must* stay in the home.
- The Health/Family area can cause exhaustion for some people (probably those who are already prone to it). Wood is the element in this area, and the purpose of the fireplace is to destroy wood. This includes even a gas fireplace.

If you have a fireplace in any of these areas, it would be a good idea to change the vibration to make it less Wood-destroying. If there are months during which it isn't used, clean it well and remove all the fireplace implements. If the fireplace is in the Health and Family area, remove most metal objects from around it. Remember, Metal is a destroyer of Wood (see Elemental Cycles). Add items that make it seem as if things grow there:

- Put real or artificial plants in or around the fireplace.
- Put pictures of growing trees around that area.
- Add a fountain right in the fireplace.
- Put seashells or other representations of water around it.
- Put pottery items around it. Pottery is made from earth. Earth and water can destroy fire, and they are required for wood to grow.

Do not place a couch directly facing a fireplace unless you use the fireplace often. Angle it somewhat, or place it perpendicular to the fireplace. If you're not going to be using a fireplace, feel free to ignore it when deciding where to put your furniture.

There is an interesting modern design technique for screening a fireplace. Put a large, well-framed picture on the hearth and lean it in front of the fireplace.

Woodburning stoves do not have most of the feng shui problems of a fireplace. They seal tightly, and even those with glass fronts don't tend to invite chi up and out. The small pottery Mexican stoves (chiminea) with an open front do, however, have the same problems as a regular fireplace, but to a lesser degree. If possible, keep a growing plant on or near your woodstove during the months when it is not used.

SPLIT-LEVEL HOUSES

The caution about split-level houses is that they can symbolize splitting up or breaking apart. Split-levels can feel awkward when they don't seem to work naturally with the landform of the lot. Often the split-level design is used as a novelty with no reference to the slope of the land.

If there is a landing directly inside the front door, hang a crystal up high in the center of the landing. A chandelier is fine if that works with your style. Find some way to draw the eye toward the living room and the feet will follow. Then you are not presenting chi with the question, "Which way is the living room?"

KITCHENS

For most people, the layout of the major kitchen appliances is unchangeable. Range tops and ovens are sometimes installed in separate places. It is best if neither of them is in a direct line opposite the sink or refrigerator. The stove represents fire. The sink and refrigerator represent water, and since water destroys fire, the area between the appliances takes on a vibration of conflict. This vibration can create a dynamic of conflict in the lives of the residents. Hang a crystal (or windchimes) between the stove and any *water* appliance that is directly opposite it. The same conflicting dynamic can come into play when a sink or refrigerator is located within a few inches of a *fire* appliance (stove, microwave, toaster oven, or toaster). If it is a small appliance, do whatever you can to move it further from the water. Sometimes a stove is located right next to the refrigerator. Common sense argues against such an arrangement, and so does feng shui. In this case, put a sheet of shiny metal (aluminum, stainless, or copper) on the side of the refrigerator to create a real and symbolic separation. If the sink, stove, and refrigerator are all in a straight line, and the stove is in the middle, it is considered to portend sadness. If the oven door opens directly in line with the entrance to the kitchen, so that you can look right into the oven when it is open, it suggests that chi will walk right in and burn right up. Hang a crystal either over the stove or directly over the cook standing at the stove.

Skylights are not good directly over stoves, because the chi from the food can vanish up and out. In this case, put a crystal, windchimes, or mobile in the skylight over the stove. Imagine a very small bagua grid applied to your stovetop. If there is a burner that isn't working well, look at that part of your life, and don't be surprised to see the problem echoed. No matter where the stove is located, it always represents money. Cleaning it is no one's favorite chore, but if it is cleaned well on a regular basis, your bank account will receive an energetic boost. Don't use just one or two stove burners on a regular basis. Try to rotate their use, so that they are all used somewhat equally. Other suggestions about stove placement are in the section on Empowered Positions in Chapter 2.

A sink usually has a small lip of counter under which you can discretely put a line of red tape. This will keep the sink from affecting a Fire appliance across from it.

Many feng shui teachers have no opinion about what sinks are made of, but stainless steel is favored by some. I like stainless steel because it's easier on glass and pottery dishes. Gas stove tops are generally preferred to electric, because the actual flame is there, doing the cooking. There is a common tendency to over-clutter the outside surfaces of the refrigerator with magnets, giving it a "bulletin board" effect. A minimal amount of "bulletin boarding" on the fridge is probably not a problem, as long as it is neat, and current, and doesn't get out of hand. If you like to put snapshots or postcards on the fridge, use the clear plastic holders that are magnetic on the back. If your refrigerator is in the Fortunate Blessings corner, it would be best not to do "bulletin boarding" at all. Instead keep the fridge front cleaned and buffed. (A very occasional application of car wax would even be helpful.) The basic idea is that the fridge surface should be easy to clean, no matter which gua it is located in.

Do not have too many small appliances stored out on the countertop in view at all times. "Too many" is a bit subjective, depending on the size of the kitchen. Anything more than three should definitely be questioned. Perhaps if you use an appliance less than three times a week, it could be stored in a cabinet. If an appliance is clean and well maintained, it aids whichever gua it is located in within the kitchen. The trick is not to have too many out in view. It is also not a good idea to have appliances that *cut*, such as can openers or food processors in the Relationship area of the kitchen. As mentioned earlier, open knife blades are a bad idea in this area as well. Cutting implements in a Relationship area can bring that dynamic into your relationships. Also don't store knives, in view, right next to the stovetop. That symbolizes *double* danger. Knives in a drawer next to the stove are fine.

If a bathroom is located directly over a kitchen, a small mirror should be affixed to the kitchen ceiling. The shiny side should be upward, and it should be on that part of the ceiling that is directly under the bathroom. If you are able to be even more specific, locate it right under the toilet.

HOME OFFICES

Home offices are best located in the front part of the house. The front half of a house partakes of a yang "come and go" energy, and offices benefit from that. Be careful that your desk is not overly large. Desks with very large surface areas can tend to "call in" that much work to do, and you may find yourself much busier than you want to be. This is definitely a case of "be careful what you ask for, because you're going to get it." I know someone with three desks in her office and each one is piled high with work to do. She thinks of herself as frantically busy.

The bagua grid can be applied to your desk. Where you sit is the entrance, and the far right corner is the Relationship area. Telephones are very appropriate in the Relationship area, as well as a photo of you and a loved one, or a photo of several people you are close to (e.g. a family photo). This is also a good area for a stack of letter trays, symbolizing relationship. Do not put things that cut in that area, such as scissors, letter openers, and staplers. Sharp things are fine in the Fame area because they have angles that symbolize Fire. Just be careful not to place pens, pencils, and scissors in such a way that they point at you. Otherwise, you are putting poison arrows on your own desk.

If your work involves creativity, do have at least one round or curvy object on your desk, preferably in the Creativity area. There is not much you can do in the three entrance guas (Knowledge, Career, Travel) of a desk. Those areas are usually very work-intensive. If, however, you can place a large black writing pad in the middle close to you, it will help to keep you on track. The far left corner is of course very important, because it is Fortunate Blessings. Things that would help in this area are a plant or flowers, a blue, purple, or red object such as a paperweight, or anything expensive such as a computer. A rounded clear crystal paperweight is considered to represent focus, and is good anywhere on a desk. You can cut pieces of colored paper, representing the appropriate shapes and colors of the bagua areas, and tape them *under* your desktop.

The door to the office should not be directly opposite the door to a bathroom. If it is, keep the bathroom door closed and hang a clear crystal between the two doors.

BEDROOMS

Bedrooms are best located in the back part of a dwelling because of the more restful yin energy there. Also for the sake of preserving restful energy, a bedroom should have only one door connecting it to the rest of the house, so that it can't be used as a hallway.

It is usually preferable to locate a child's bedroom in other areas than the Fortunate Blessings area of the dwelling. Another name for this area is Empowerment, and if the children are too empowered, they'll rule the roost. If having a child's bedroom in this area is unavoidable, try to have a picture of the parents visible in that room. If a bedroom is located directly over a garage, on the next level above it, those who sleep in that room may not be getting their best quality sleep. Some things that you can do to aid restful sleep in this situation are:

- Put very heavy solid objects on the floor of the bedroom. Two examples would be a sculpture or a table with a heavy stone base.
- Hang a crystal over the car in the garage. Yes, this can be done even if the garage door opens upward—just use ingenuity.
- Put a mirror (any kind, any size) on the ceiling of the garage, reflecting the top of the car.

If a bedroom is directly behind a garage, there is a similar problem, since the "metal beast" is pointed directly at a sleep area and undue pressure could be felt in that person's life. Place a mirror on the back wall of the garage, so that it reflects the front of the car away from the bedroom. In both situations involving bedrooms and garages, there is not a problem for sleepers if cars are never parked in the garage.

Bedrooms that extend away from the bulk of the house in a somewhat *solitary* way indicate that whoever sleeps in that room may not feel wholly connected to the rest of the household. Put a mirror on the bedroom wall that is adjoining the rest of the house. The mirror should face into the bedroom. This will symbolically draw that room back into the house.

If a kitchen is located directly over a bedroom it is recommended that a small mirror be placed on the ceiling of the bedroom, reflecting up. The mirror symbolically seals off and pushes away the bustling kitchen vibrations from the quiet bedroom. The mirror can be tiny; even one inch will work.

It is best if a bedroom does not have a door that opens directly into a bathroom. There are plenty of homes that break this rule. If there is a door between the bedroom and the bathroom, that door should always be kept closed at night when you are sleeping. The moist, "body waste" energy of the bathroom should not be able to flow around you in your dreamtime. There is an architectural fad that was popularized by the so-called "monster homes." Master bedroom suites are thought to be luxurious if there is no door between the sleeping area and the bath area. If you own such a home, put in a solid (not louvered) door. If that cannot be easily done, put up curtains, even sheers. The curtains can stay open until you are ready for sleep.

Feng shui does not recommend having a television in the bedroom. If you truly have no other place for your television, I suggest that you place it within a cabinet that can be closed, or else drape fabric over it when it is not in use. This will symbolically close the eye of the television—turning it off is not enough. If the bedroom is for a couple, it would be best if the television were out of there—period. When the television goes on, human relating usually stops.

The constantly open eyes of plush animals and dolls can be a factor in the restless sleep of many people, especially children. Because the eyes don't usually close, they are awake all night long. Pictures on display in bedrooms should also be peaceful.

Some people have no choice but to locate their desk in their bedroom. While certainly not ideal, this *can* work (from a feng shui viewpoint) if the desk area can be visually screened or curtained from the bed at sleep time. If you have exercise equipment in your bedroom, it should also be visually screened when not in use. Exercise and deskwork are the opposite of "sleep energy."

CEILING

If a ceiling is below eight feet, it can feel too low. The space can feel cramped. Paint it white so it feels more expansive, and use uplights—lights that shine upward. They lift the oppressive energy. Most average-height ceilings should be white or a very light shade (usually of the wall color).

Ceilings can also be too high and not contain the energy in the room well. Rooms with ceilings higher than ten feet (and in some cases twelve feet) can have an "unsettled" energy. Loft homes and McMansions (extremely large suburban houses) often have overly high ceilings in the living room areas. Very high ceilings are more suited for businesses than homes. Paint them a bit darker than usual to make them seem lower. Also, if you can, install crown molding around the walls some distance below the ceiling. Paint the wall above the molding the same color as the ceiling.

In rooms with high ceilings, most of the artificial light should be directed downward, making cozy pools of light on the floor. The furniture should be dark, substantial, and heavy-looking to ground energy.

ROOF

Overhanging roofs represent protection. Every (free-standing) home's roof should overhang the outside *front* wall. It is preferred that all the outside walls of the home have some roof hanging over them. If there is none, perhaps add a faux mansard roof with overhang.

A-frame houses have the roof going all the way to the ground. From a feng shui viewpoint, that's quite extreme for a home. The upper floors especially feel pinched in the head area, and that's not a good place to feel pinched. Paint the inside of the roof white, and hang a large clear crystal from the inside peak of the roof.

HIGH-RISE APARTMENTS AND CONDOS

If you live above the fourth floor, I advise you to use a magnetic sleep pad under your mattress (see Sources.) You should also have some heavy, and I do mean *heavy*, objects on the floor of your home. Stone statues, or tables supported by marble, are two suggestions. Whatever the color of your floor or rugs, it should be a rather dark hue.

High-rise units often have too many windows and they often have windows directly opposite the entrance door. Both indicate a failure to sufficiently retain chi energy, which is covered in Chapter 2. The best *real* solution is to use sheer curtains. The *symbolic* solutions are to place crystals or windchimes in the windows or to put a tiny mirror (shining in) near the windows.

AIR CIRCULATION

The ideal building has good natural air circulation, such as windows that open. If your home has areas with stagnant air, install a quiet fan. If parts of your home are much cooler than other parts, and thereby not lived in as much, install a gentle heater (such as a baseboard heater) to make the temperature more even throughout the home. Even temperature and good air circulation go a long way toward making a home support you in a holistic way.

Also, be aware of echoes in your home. They signify emptiness. Consider hanging a rug, tapestry, or quilt to absorb some of the sound.

Chapter 7:

Furniture and Household Objects

BEDS

The ideal feng shui bed has nothing stored under it, has a solid (probably wood) headboard, and a footboard that isn't taller than the bedspread. Obviously, most folks don't have the ideal, so here's what to do. If things *must* be stored under the bed, those things should be emotionally "quiet"—no old tax records, no old diaries. Clothes and bedding are rarely a problem, since they get laundered regularly, washing away old vibes. It is best not to be able to see under a bed, so use a bed skirt or something similar.

A solid headboard is helpful for anyone, but it is imperative for a monogamous relationship bed. A headboard with bars or slats says "open relationship" and can never hold a relationship together as well as a solid headboard. Be wary of headboards that have a high overhead shelf built in. Preferably, put nothing on that shelf (over your head) except perhaps plant vines twining together. Don't let the actual plant pots be over your head area—they should be off to the side.

A headboard backs you up, and a footboard gives you grounding. If a footboard is not feasible or desired, do try to put something at the foot of your bed to represent a grounding. Suggestions are a cedar chest, a bench, or even a dark-colored blanket placed at the end of your bed.

The only beds that should be sitting directly on the floor are beds that are designed that way, such as folding foam mattresses. Box springs and the like should always be up and off the floor.

A king-sized bed poses a problem to a permanent relationship because the mattress is usually placed upon two separate box springs (twin width). Because the box springs are closer to the floor, they are more fundamental. This reinforces the basic differences between the two partners. Replacing the bed with a queen-sized bed is a perfect solution, because it draws the people physically closer together. If that isn't a workable solution for you, then get a red king-sized sheet, and place it between the box springs and the mattress. Try to find a brilliant red sheet, because it symbolizes a new "blood" foundation.

Bunk beds should only be used if there is absolutely no alternative. If they must be used do not let the structural support beneath the upper mattress (the metal links) be visible to the person in the lower bunk. Perhaps use fabric with a star pattern to cover it.

GLASS TABLETOPS

When chi is busily scooting and scurrying around your house, it would be best if it didn't run into a glass tabletop. The chi will get sliced and the effect will be to cut you off from reaching your goals and potential. Imagine a glass Frisbee with a razor-sharp edge sailing around the room. If the glass tabletop has a rim around it, such as wood or metal, the slicing effect does not happen and all is well. Some glass stores will have a metallic tape with a faux finish. It sticks to the edge of the glass but doesn't work well on a sharp beveled edged. It is not cheap, but it looks quite good and can quickly make a table more feng-shui friendly.

If a table (with exposed glass rim) is very central, such as a coffee table or dining table, the effect is severe. If the table is away in some corner or if it's an obscure glass shelf, the effect can be quite minimal. Glass shelves which are higher than your head are probably nothing to be concerned about, at least from a feng shui point of view.

When I was first learning feng shui I heard this caution about bare glass edges, but I didn't want to believe it, because I had two glass shelves in the Fame area of my home and I thought they looked great. I kept studying and kept hearing the same advice "Don't have them!" Finally one day I threw my hands up and decided to give it a try. I wrapped the glass in paper and put them in a closet. Very soon thereafter I got my website, and Elaine Gill of The Crossing Press *asked me* to write this book! I got rid of the glass shelves permanently and have never looked back. What I tell people now is to just give it a try (cover the glass or put it away) and see if you don't like the *result* in your life better than you liked the bare glass edge.

ALTARS

An altar is a visual representation of a person's spiritual aspiration. Some people have no altars, some people have one, and some people have altars everywhere. If you do have an altar, here are some tips:

- Things that are very appropriate on an altar are a central image, a light source, flowers or a plant, a symbolic offering (such as water or fruit), and an incense holder.
- Try to have the central image at least as high as your heart (when standing). Many people have very low altars, and often the reason is that they don't have a higher table. Feel free to use a wall shelf.
- In most cases, it is a good idea to have the central image on some sort of upraised platform (a plinth). This could be a slab of stone or a wooden box, sometimes covered with beautiful fabric such as brocade. A plinth is a very respectful way of giving visual importance to a central image.
- Do not let your altar become cluttered. Clutter means hard to clean well, and an altar should be nicely clean. It should not be a collecting place for crystals, special rocks, shells, feathers, and so forth. Your attention should be immediately drawn to the main image. It can then act as a powerful centering device in your life—visual teaching.
- A small altar need not have formal symmetry. One candle (on the right side of the altar as you are facing it) and one vase of flowers (on the left side) are enough to bring appropriate visual balance.
- A larger altar might have a balanced triad of images with candles and flowers on each side. At the risk of stating the obvious, I will say that the candleholders should match each other and the vases should match each other. An offering dish should be directly in front of the central image and the incense holder in front of that (closest to you).
- If you are using stick incense, the incense holder should allow the stick to be placed vertically. This symbolizes your attentive attitude. A dish of sand works fine.
- If there is a mirror on the wall directly behind the altar, either remove the mirror, or cover it with beautiful fabric.
- If the altar is in a bedroom, position it so that the bottoms of your feet are not pointing directly at it. It is not considered respectful. If there is no alternative, then perhaps you could have a footboard on your bed.

Be aware of what you are giving visual importance, and what it might symbolize. You can be giving an aspect of your home an "altar-like" vibe by excessively formalizing it. A common example might be the décor around some very formal fireplaces. Please note what you may be making an altar to. You may unconsciously be giving chi energy a message.

Many people like to pray and/or meditate in front of their altars. There is nothing wrong with that, but if you do, I suggest that you have another, much plainer spot where the majority of your quiet spiritual practice takes place. I recommend meditating or praying with your eyes barely open, looking slightly in front of you. Spiritual activity is a time of deep centering. A simple, clean blank wall (in front of you) serves as an admirable aid in mediation and prayer.

CLOCKS

If there is a clock in your home that isn't working, it should be repaired. It is stuck at some time in the past, and is causing that same dynamic to happen to you. Even clocks in storage will have that effect to some degree. They hold you back and keep you from reaching your goals. Stoves with built-in clocks can be especially problematic, because the stove is so powerful. Very often the clock stops working decades before the stove. Of course the best thing is to have it repaired, but if you are a renter, the cost may seem prohibitive. I would suggest using tape to cover over the clock as neatly as possible, then buying a small timer if you have been using the built-in one.

A working clock acts as an energetic boost to any area in which it is located. If the clock has noticeable movement, such as a pendulum, so much the better. If any adult in the home finds a ticking clock to be obnoxious, honor that and replace the clock with a silent one.

Analog clocks (clocks with moving hands) are a bit easier on the brain than digital clocks (which just have numbers), because they require less interpretation. The movement of the hands relates to the natural movement of the sun in the sky. This is not to say they are better in every situation, but generally they make a room more peaceful than digital clocks do.

MIRRORS

Mirrors have many uses in feng shui, and are frequently recommended. They indicate how truly and honestly you see yourself. They should always be clean and in good repair—no cracks, no bad silvering. A cracked mirror gives you a fractured image of yourself, as do mirror tiles. There is a recent fad of having mirrors inside the mullions of a window frame. The only time one of those mirrors would be acceptable would be if it were placed high enough so that no one in the house is reflected in it.

Old mirrors with bad silvering cannot give you a true reflection of yourself, and can contribute to low self-esteem. In the case of an antique, the bad silvering actually adds to the value of the piece, and if that's the reason you own it, here's what to do. Have the old glass removed, save it, and replace it with new mirror glass. If and when you sell the piece, put the bad mirror back in, and the value is preserved, but you haven't had to live with the consequences of it for all those years. Incidentally, new mirror glass is incredibly cheap. If you have a mirror (usually a bathroom mirror) with bad silvering only along the bottom, the reason is that the cleaning liquid has been allowed to drip to the bottom before being wiped. When any liquid (even condensed water) drips to the bottom of a mirror, it wicks under to the back side and corrodes the silvering.

Also, mirrors of smoked or colored glass should to be avoided. Some mirrors have designs etched or painted on them. It is best not to have such mirrors in your home, but if you already have one and want to keep it, put it at such a height where no one is reflected in it. If the design is just around the border, the mirror can be used anywhere.

You (and every adult residing in your home) should be able to fully see your face when standing in front of any mirror (which is intended for that purpose). If not all of your head can be seen you may experience problems such as headaches or unclear thinking. Ideally a mirror should show the space eight inches above your head, because that represents your potential. It's also good to be able to see at least half of your throat, where your words come from.

Mirrors give the illusion of expanding a space, and this property is useful any time you feel the need to symbolically enlarge a tight area. This also lets you "bring in" fresh energy to any gua in which a mirror is placed.

It is important to be aware of what a mirror is reflecting, because it is symbolically doubling that view. It would be best not to reflect clutter, toilets, or *bottoms* of stairs. There is one seemingly odd exception to mirrors reflecting toilets. Many feng shui teachers recommend putting a small mirror *on the ceiling* reflecting directly down onto the toilet. I consider this especially important to do if the toilet is in the Center or Fortunate Blessings area of the residence.

Mirrors are used for quite a few different purposes in feng shui. They are able to seal off certain undesirable vibrations, such as from bathrooms. Mirrors can also symbolically bring back missing areas. Mirrors are superb for repelling menacing energy. They reflect it back on itself. Occasionally they are used to move a view from one wall to its opposite wall.

Do not use convex or concave mirrors to view yourself on a regular basis, unless you need the enlargement for something like shaving or makeup application.

SYMBOLISM

Feng shui takes symbolism quite seriously and literally. Be cautious of these kinds of symbols in your home:

- One of the things that can affect you is representations (pictures or statues) of bodies with missing parts (such as the Venus de Milo). Sooner or later, that symbolism will begin to have a detrimental effect on your health. A statue of a head without a body may or may not be problematic. If the statue looks as if it were originally intended to be only a head (such as a bust of Nefertiti or Shakespeare), there is no problem. But if the neck looks jagged as if it were lopped off a larger statue (as is the case with many Buddha heads), it retains some of that vibration of vandalism.
- The situation is much the same with representations of ruins. Such symbols say that your glory years are a thing of the past. It is best to part with such objects.
- Masks can be problematic in several ways:

  —The most obvious thing about a mask is that it is hiding the real you.
  —The expression or facial features are important to consciously recognize. Question how they represent you or your family. It may not be bad, but at least *think about* what it means.
  —If the mask is an old ethnic mask and was used shamanistically, it can sometimes have a very strong effect on people (maybe yourself?) The overlay of vibrations because of its ceremonial use can be powerful.

- Dead flowers, which symbolize stagnation.
- The simple symbolism of a home that is visually over-cluttered says that the life of the resident (or residents) will seem busy or hectic.
- Pictures of your ex-relationship partner should not be on display if you are seeking a new relationship. By putting those pictures away in a scrapbook you are symbolically making room for someone new.

- A drain is a drain is a drain. It can symbolize energy and money draining out of your life. A drain is a hole in what would otherwise be a solid wall or floor. The hole is seen as a weakness in that solid surface.

- Waterfall pictures that use light and electricity to make the water seem like it's moving are a problem. The symbol is fire under water and symbolizes conflict.

- Crackled glass surfaces can bring the vibration of "breaking up" into a home. I feng shui'd for a married couple who had just moved into a home with a dining table and built-in breakfast bar, both of which were made of glass that looked like someone had taken a sledgehammer to a car windshield. I was puzzled when I saw it because it didn't even *look* stable. I cautioned them about it and the husband agreed, but the wife told me it was the "latest thing" and she wouldn't dream of changing it. Their marriage lasted a few more months.

LIVING ROOM FURNISHINGS

The furniture in your living room should look inviting. Imagine a chair or couch to be people. As you enter the room, they've either got their arms open to you or their back to you. Open arms are welcoming. If the back of a chair, and especially a couch, is first presented when entering a room it symbolizes a chilly reception—people with their backs to the guests coming in. Try to arrange the seating so that you don't have to walk around it to sit in it. Make it easy to walk into the room.

When arranging the main furniture of the living room, it is important not to put large seats (couches) *directly* across from each other. It would be better to angle them somewhat. Couches directly facing each other can say "opposing positions" and create disharmony.

If the living area and dining area are together in one large undivided room, it's time to think about a room divider. (An L-shaped room counts as an undivided area.) The divider should preferably be quite real, as in tall shelving, cabinets, or decorative screens. If that won't work in your situation, try a couple of tall plants, graciously announcing the entrance to the dining area.

Chapter 8:

Other Considerations

YIN/YANG

The yin yang symbolizes a very basic Taoist concept—balance—a balance that changes, but stays balanced. In computer language, it's either zero or one. In Taoism, it's either yin or yang. Just about everything imaginable can be divided between these two. If it isn't divided hard-line, it is somewhere on a scale between very yin and very yang. Some of the concepts that apply to interiors are divided thusly:

YIN	YANG
Lower part of a room	Upper part of a room
Private	Public
Moist	Dry
Dark	Light
Many things	Few things
Complex	Simple
Feminine	Masculine
Cold	Hot
Soft	Hard
Quiet	Loud

Indoors	Outdoors
Stillness	Movement
Death	Life
Horizontal	Vertical
Sleep	Awake
Closed and Tight	Open and Expansive

The bathroom is the most yin room in the home. It has no stove or oven to help balance the several areas of wetness (tub, shower, sinks, and toilet). If a bathroom is visually busy or complicated, the yin component is pushed off the scale, and the room becomes very out of balance and not so healthy. To alleviate this, keep it simple—almost austere. A bathroom can be elegant and feel wonderful if you simply use color as the uniting theme. Use the appropriate bagua colors, depending on where the bathroom is in the house. Bring those colors into the room through the towels, bathmats, shower curtain, soap dish, or soap squirter. Don't try to apply the whole bagua to a bathroom. The space is really just too small to make effective statements for each of the nine guas. Instead, if the bathroom is in the Creativity area of the house, go for chrome and pastels. If it is in the Relationship area of the house, go for pinks, reds, and whites, and groupings of things. The bathroom is often decorated with water imagery—seashells, pictures of the ocean, et cetera. Once again, this makes the room too yin. Only if a bathroom were in the Life's Path area would I recommend *any* water imagery, preferably a picture of a flowing stream or river. If the bathroom is in any other part of the house, do not add water imagery to an already wet room.

Note that yang is public, and yin is private and quiet. A home is naturally a more yin place than a store. However, a home can be too yin (or have parts that are too yin—any room that is mostly unused). Examples are:

- A home that is directly next door to a building that is not used on a daily basis (such as churches).
- A home wherein a pet is left alone all day, and the animal spends many of its hours listless and somber. That vibration continues to affect the dwelling.
- A home with a bedridden person.

LOT SHAPE

Feng shui prefers regularly shaped lots—four sides in either a square or a rectangle—for a balanced life. Any lot with a very bizarrely shaped map outline is not advisable. Triangular lots are the most extreme, having only three sides. The message is that something is likely to be very missing in your life. The very worst triangular shape is one with a tight acute angle. See Fig. 30. And if bad weren't bad enough, it could get worse. The worst scenario is where the front door faces directly toward a tight, narrow corner of the lot. It suggests that things could get tighter for you in the future. The larger a lot is, the less of a problem its triangular shape is.

Triangular lot shapes

Horrible lot shape   **Even worse**

Fig. 30

If the property will be used *only* commercially, it's not likely to be a severe problem. The busy yang nature of commercial use can overcome bad lot shape. If the triangular lot contains multiple apartments or condominiums, it is almost certainly not a problem at all. The unit you live in is yours, but the lot is not.

Lights, mirrors, and good landscaping are your choices for solutions:

- Round out the tight corners of the lot with plantings that give the impression that the lot shape is squarer.
- Put mirrors (usually small) at the edge of your property, near the corners, facing into your property. They symbolically expand the property. The mirror can be small, and it should face in toward your property. You can put it on a small metal stake, such as hardware stores sell for holding reflectors.
- Try to light up any tight corners on your lot. It symbolically expands them. An electric light on a pole is the usual recommendation, but it

can sometimes look awkward. Solar lights are good, as are the little lights on a string. Any light is better than no light. The light needs to function and be used at least occasionally.

- If that seems like a waste of electricity, *let nature make light for you*. Plants with white variegation on the leaves make an area feel lighter and therefore more open. On moonlit nights the area *glows* very noticeably. Ask a nursery or landscape consultant which white variegated plants will do well in your climate. Variegated plants are in all sizes from low ground covers to mighty trees.
- If the front door is facing a tight corner, put a mirror outside the front door, facing away from the house. A bagua mirror would be best. The mirror pushes the tight energy away from the home.

There is one lot shape that is an improvement over a square or a rectangle. It is a trapezoid with the back side larger than the front side. See Fig. 31. It symbolizes a drawstring purse, with coins dropped into the entrance and adding up and bulging in the bottom. The back of the lot is the bottom of the moneybag. It holds good fortune well. Good fortune can come in many forms including money. These kinds of lots are called "moneybag lots."

Lots that are the opposite shape, with a larger entrance side and a smaller back side, are not auspicious. They're called "dustpan lots" and they suggest good fortune will be pinched. Try to avoid buying that shape property, and if you are living on one, I suggest landscaping to make the lot appear more regular (square or rectangular).

Moneybag lot shape (outline)

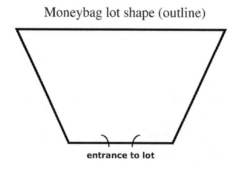

entrance to lot

Fig. 31

A corner of a lot is pinched any time the angle is more acute than ninety degrees. The severity of the problem depends on the narrowness of the angle. A sharper corner is more of a problem than a corner that is closer to ninety degrees. The challenge is to make the area feel more open. Use any of the first four solutions listed above for triangular lots.

Remember that a moneybag lot doesn't usually need remedies in any of its corners. Do them if you want to, but the power of the *entire lot shape* is the main dynamic on that property.

Good fortune symbolically accumulates behind a house. If the back yard is too small, good fortune has a hard time accumulating. "Too small" is judged in relation to the front yard. The back yard should be as big as, or a bit bigger than, the front yard. If the back yard is drastically smaller than the front yard, think twice about moving into that house. That dynamic is going to be tough, and it may not be possible to fix it completely. If the back yard is tiny, and enclosed by a wood fence, consider putting a large mirror on the fence. It will really make the property seem larger. Another solution is to paint a trompe-l'oeil on the back yard fence. That is, a scene with depth of perspective. This too will make the back yard seem larger.

REPAIRS AND RENOVATIONS

Repairs

Repairs and renovations mean very different things to renters and to homeowners. Not every owner of rental property is conscientious. If you are a renter, please be assertive when repairs are due to your home. Be the squeaky wheel that gets the oil! Note the area of the bagua that is in need of repair. That aspect of your life is probably "getting clobbered."

It would be nice if all windows opened fully, but many are painted shut. The importance of fully functioning windows is discussed in Chapter 6. Unstick those windows, even if you have to hire someone. Do this even if you are a renter! You're the one living there—you will receive the benefit.

Renovations

The feng shui view of major home renovation is that you are operating on a body. Proceed with care. The results can be great or horrible. I recommend talking to the space that is going to be disturbed, explaining what is going to be done, and why. Give it advance warning, and perhaps say, "You'll like it" or something similar.

When creating additions to your home, it would be best to "fill in" any missing areas. Be sure not to totally enclose a bathroom—that would be a huge mistake! There is no universal agreement in the feng shui world as to which is better—an addition making a house deeper or an addition making a house wider. See Fig. 32. I almost always recommend deeper, because it adds depth and resonance to the occupants' lives. By making a house wider, you are increasing people's ability to be further removed from each other (and they will be). Never make the second floor of a house seem larger than the first floor, as this can bring an instability to its residents. Viewed from the front, a house should look balanced, left and right. Renovations can create or accentuate that "balanced look." If you have the opportunity to create a "bulge" in your Fortunate Blessings area, do so. You will never look back! When a new space has been created within a home, I recommend singing or chanting within that space to welcome it, energetically connecting it to the rest of the house.

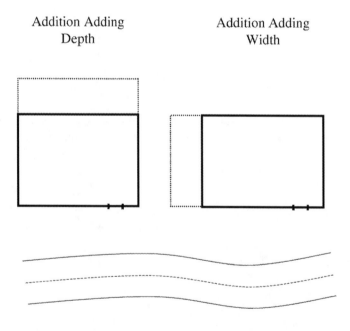

Fig. 32

DETAILS

The bad news is that feng shui does indeed pay attention to the very small details. They may be small, but they do exist, and they do convey a message. The good news is that you can control that message by going ahead fixing or cleaning or organizing whatever details in your physical environment that you've been intending to do. (Yes, this could involve making a list.) Attend to those details and you'll have your home humming a happy tune. I realize that saying it is often easier than doing it, but details matter.

If you have hardback books with dust covers on them, realize that they have a more settled vibe if the dust covers are stored separately, out of sight. The publishers of hardback books frequently provide nicely embossed covers (sometimes of real fabric) with the book. Take advantage of the visual beauty that you may already own and enjoy the cloth covers. But remove the covers only if sunlight never reaches the books. Sunlight will fade the books. Don't throw the dustcovers away, because they are frequently 90% of the books' monetary value. (I file the dustcovers in a file box in alphabetical order by title.)

Take the time to set all the grooves in the heads of the screws in the switch plate and electrical socket covers identically. If you set them vertically throughout the house, you are tilting the scale a bit more in the yang direction because vertical is a more yang and active direction than horizontal. If all the screws are already nicely set horizontally, that's fine too—it's just more yin, and represents Earth which is good. The fact that they are all the same is the main thing. It simplifies the look, shows that somebody cared, and helps to prevent a vibe of chaos from setting in. The switch plate screws are especially important because they are usually closer to eye level. If they might get rusty replace them with inexpensive nylon screws.

Don't have nails or hooks anywhere inside or outside the home that are no longer used for anything. Take them down and spackle the hole. They represent "psychic hooks"—something from the past that keeps catching you.

I had a client who was a legal secretary in downtown Oakland. The building was classic Art Deco and her offices had beautiful old wood paneling with lots of trim. I had consulted for her home a few weeks earlier, and when I got to her office I noted that she had already put a fountain the right place and plants in the right places. I was almost at a loss for what to say until I noticed how dusty the paneling was, and that there were zillions of little pieces of clear tape stuck to the paneling. I asked about it and she said that the person who had occupied the office before her had taped things to the wall everywhere. I suggested that she either hire someone who knew how to do detailed cleaning or that she take the time to do it herself. Bless her heart, she did it herself, and about three days later she left a message on my answering machine that I have saved to this day because of the enthusiasm in her voice. "I just had to share with you. Since you were here on Saturday I have had two people come in and *cheerfully* pay me things that have been overdue now for *two years!* I thought I would *never* collect on those, and actually they came in and cheerfully paid me not only what they owed me, but extra because they felt guilty. I just can't believe it! Thank you so much for helping me with my office! Have a great day, I'm certainly having one!" The bills that were overdue were old stuck energy and they were represented by the pieces of old tape stuck on her walls.

All this isn't to say that there can't be someplace in your home that isn't thoroughly perfect and organized. Even the greatest feng shui masters say that trying for 100% perfect feng shui is not the desired goal. There are other factors in your life such as your education, friends, and life choices. Don't use feng shui as an excuse to drive yourself (or your partner) crazy—anything can be overdone.

GUESTS

Yourself as a Guest:

- If you are staying in any form of public lodging you can easily make your stay more feng shui-friendly. Ask for your room to be in the rear half of the facility and away from elevators. Just before going to bed, cover any and all poison arrows that are aiming at the bed. I recommend covering them just before going to bed (towels are fine) and removing the covers as soon as you rise. That way your place doesn't look weird. A television only *needs* to be covered when you are sleeping, but feel free to cover it any time you want. The bathroom door should be closed when you are sleeping.

- If you are staying with friends, exactly the same principles apply, except that you probably won't have a choice about the location of the guestroom. Do be sensitive not to inadvertently offend your host as you make your place more feng shui-friendly. Remember, poison arrows that aim at a bed only have to be covered while you are in the bed. Receive your guest lodgings with gratitude. Feng shui highly approves of the old courtesy of expressing your appreciation by sending a "thank you" card when you have arrived home.

Guests in Your Home:

- If you have a guestroom in your home, but it is seldom used, it may be too yin. Any room can become too yin by being underused or undervisited. Notice where the guestroom is in the bagua of your whole house. The corresponding area of your life may be rather inactive. The best solution I know of is to simply *use that room.* Do *something* in there on a regular basis. A small decorative light on a timer set to come on for a few hours in the evening is another option. If your guest room also doubles as an office, which is increasingly popular, cover the unused computer screens while a guest is staying in the room. A nice fabric, perhaps.
- If you don't have a guestroom, then plan so that your guest's possessions don't clutter any guas that you are working on. My friend Sally let a friend stay with her for a week. Sally was living in a very nicely maintained studio apartment, and she knew enough about feng shui to know where the different bagua areas were. But without thinking she let her friend's things go into the Relationship area of her apartment. During that one week, Sally said that basically all the relationships in her life "fell apart," resulting in her moving away. One of the best ways to make a guest feel welcome is to provide horizontal space for them to place their things, such as tables and drawers. Such a place would ideally:
    —Feel secure and somewhat private
    —Not be in the Wealth or Relationship guas.

Occasionally think of yourself as a guest in your own home. Do be grateful. At some point in time you will permanently leave your dwelling. Rare is the person who is born and dies in the same house. In a sense, we are all visitors to the dwellings that shelter us. We should endeavor to leave them cleaner and nicer than when we arrived. Otherwise we will probably accrue some "bad karma." Treat your home well—maintain it, and keep it clean. If you can train yourself to develop the ability to *truly* see your home as a visitor might, you've gained a valuable feng shui skill.

CARS

A basic feng shui rule is that the more time you spend in a particular place, the more you are affected by that place. The more you are in a particular car, the more it affects you. Definitely if you sleep in your car, it is affecting you a lot. An object that changes direction as frequently as a car does not lend itself to compass-oriented feng shui. Entrance-based bagua is the only method to use on most cars. The mouth of chi (or entrance) is where you open the hood to access the motor. So, if you open the front hood to get to the motor, your Fortunate Blessings area includes the back left bumper and some of the interior of the trunk, and some of the left back seat area. Cars with no back seat often have none of the Fortunate Blessings in the "people part" of the car. If the engine is in the back of the car, then the mouth of chi is in the back of the car, and the bagua orientation flips around, so that the Fame area is where the hood ornament is, or would be.

When driving, it is essential to have your brain in gear. It would be preferable not to point a poison arrow right at your head with the sun visor. You can often get the same shading effect by pushing the visor outward toward the windshield. However, the *most* important thing in this case is visibility and safety.

The main guas that I recommend enhancing in a vehicle when traveling, or spending a lot of time in your vehicle, are:

- Travel/Helpful People
- Fortunate Blessings
- Relationship (if you have traveling companions).

The best way to enhance an area is to make sure it's clean and orderly.

This includes bumper stickers on the outside of a vehicle. If they have faded or are not relevant, remove them. They really aren't directing fresh chi toward whatever cause they are espousing. The result is basically the opposite of what you had desired. Remove all traces of old bumper stickers, using the proper solvent if necessary.

Bumper stickers are not objectionable if:

- They are removed well when old or faded.
- There are not too many. When there are too many they are all talking at once and have therefore lost most of their impact. Feng shui doesn't care *whether or not* you have bumper stickers, but too many is definitely a no-no.

People have different visual temperaments when it comes to hanging things from rearview mirrors or ornamenting dashboards. Many teachers recommend hanging a small, reflective silver ball from your rear view mirror. These are called mayan balls. A small crystal will enhance any area. Do more if you are inclined to do so. Do absolutely nothing that would impede visibility and safety.

OTHER VEHICLES

The model of the *engine as "mouth of chi"* for cars holds true for most other types of transportation vehicles. There is, however, another orientation of the bagua that can apply in some other vehicles.

In a camper or any vehicle that you actually sleep in, there is an additional bagua based on the door that is used to access the living area. If the driver's door and front passenger door also access the living area, then the main bagua is still the one that is based on the engine as entrance. If the living area is not accessible from the driver's area, the most influential bagua for that living area is based on its "people door." The bed of a pickup truck has a bagua that is based on the tailgate as entrance. If there is a camper shell over the bed of the truck, that particular bagua has significantly more impact because it is an enclosed space.

EMFs

Electromagnetic frequencies are a fact of life that ancient feng shui masters never had to deal with. It requires no special talent to locate electromagnetic hotspots in your home. You just need a gaussmeter, and unfortunately they're not cheap. Hopefully they will eventually be available for rent at rent-all places. Heart doctors usually have them and you might be able to borrow one. One source for meters to measure electromagnetic frequencies (as well as microwave) is AlphaLab—see Sources at the end of the book.

Especially watch out for apartments on the second or third floor where you can see electric lines within 20 feet of your windows. Measure the EMFs to be sure. Do not ever live right smack-dab next door to an electric substation. When I go by a substation in a car and my gaussmeter is on, the needle always jumps up high, and then goes back down as we drive on.

The EMFs of cell phones are of great concern because the phones are usually placed right next to your brain. Cell phones vary greatly—some are just fine and some are just horrible. Unless you know that the EMFs on your phone are low, put it on speakerphone and set the phone down while talking—then all is well. The earphone devices that I've tested seem to mostly be okay. I don't trust the websites that rate the EMFs of cell phones because the information is provided by the manufacturer, and that seems like foxes guarding henhouses. The reports on some of those websites have been at odds with the reality of my own gaussmeter tests. I've tested a huge number of cell phones and generally they *are* getting better, but if you're planning to hold a cell phone next to your head, get it tested. Some wireless household phones also have rather high EMFs. The safest phones to use are *always* those that have a wire connecting the handset to the wall.

Be aware that flat screen televisions and computers have infinitely lower EMFs than the older tube models. Laptop computers should never be placed directly on your lap. That's exactly next to your reproductive organs, and that's where the working guts of the computer are, and almost always where the highest EMFs are located. At least use a very thick pillow or a breakfast-in-bed tray to put the laptop on, raising it a few inches above your body. If you are using a pillow, place a board between the pillow and the computer so the laptop's ventilation isn't hindered.

Almost anything that is electrical and heats up has high EMFs close to it when it's turned on. Such things are hairdryers, popcorn poppers, transformers that plug into a wall socket, electric heaters, coffee grinders, electric toothbrushes, and so forth. I recommend using a blender to grind coffee instead of an electric grinder that you have to keep your hand on while it's grinding. Blenders too have high EMFs while they're on, but you can walk away from them. Electric massage devices have severe EMFs when they're turned on. This includes neck massagers, foot massagers, and massage chairs. It's my opinion that they do more harm than good. If you want a massage and don't want to pay for it, do massage exchange with someone—it's perhaps the finest use for human hands. Infrared saunas can have very high EMFs close to the heating elements. Often the only place that is safely away from those EMFs is on a separate stool placed just inside the door. Some electric blankets have extremely high EMFs and some have practically none.

There are sophisticated devices using diodes or magnets to counteract harmful frequencies. Although they are usually expensive I have not found that any of these products are effective. The only thing that is effective is a sheet of metal, such as a large cookie sheet.

Robert Becker has written several excellent books on EMFs.

Pregnancy

It is commonly believed in feng shui that if a woman lives in the same house throughout her pregnancy, the child will easily settle down for very long periods of time. This has nothing to do with how soon they move away from their parents. If a pregnant woman changes homes, the child will probably have a bit more of what we might think of as "gypsy blood." Settling down will not come as easily or naturally for that offspring.

Some feng shui authors offer a formula for getting pregnant. See *Feng Shui: Harmony by Design* in Recommended Reading. One of the recommendations is that you refrain from cleaning under your bed for the entire time that you are trying to get pregnant. I have certainly had clients who felt this was very effective for them.

ASHES

The ash remains of a loved one (human or pet) are sometimes kept at home, and people wonder if there is a better or worse place for them. As long as they are placed respectfully, they can be anywhere. The obvious exceptions are: don't have them in a laundry room, kitchen, bathroom, garage, or closet. If you're going to keep them in a closet, you might as well just return them to the earth. If they are your ancestors, perhaps have them if the Health and Family area; otherwise the Helpful People area is always appropriate.

THE NUMBER FOUR

There is absolutely nothing wrong with the number four. You may have heard that some Chinese people consider it to be an unlucky number. That is only because the Cantonese word for "four" sounds like the Cantonese word for "death." That is a very linguistically and culturally specific thing, and has nothing to do with the energetic power of four. It is a strong number, and a foursquare building is considered *ideal* in feng shui.

The sound of words that are of a language that you (perhaps) don't even understand means zero to you. Whatever your house number is, find a reason to like it. See it as a strong number.

ORGANIZING

Feng shui views organizing (and cleanliness) as *kindergarten*. They are basic—fundamental. I truthfully stress their great importance. It is nearly impossible to reach your highest potential and achieve your goals without organizing and cleanliness. Develop organizing skills. There have been hundreds of books written on organizing, but disorganized people are often the last ones who have time to read them. Audiobooks are more accessible—everybody has time to listen to a recording. You can listen while in transit, or when bathing. One of the very best audios on organizing is Stephanie Winston's *Getting Organized* (see Recommended Reading). Listening to this several times can probably cure anyone's disorganization.

Don't put obstacles in the way. Prioritize your time. You may have to be diligent to keep this as one of your highest priorities. If your abode looks helter-skelter it is not supporting you to your highest potential. It is as simple as that!

Think of everything in your space as information. That information is being heard by you and your higher self. (Please substitute whatever words feel more appropriate to you—guardian angel, guides, Universe...) What you *don't* want to be hearing (consciously or subconsciously) from your objects is, "Come here! Go there! Do this! Do that!" You also don't want to be hearing, "Don't look here," which is what you can be unconsciously saying to yourself and others when you honestly look around the room and see things like:

- Jumbles of electric cords (signifying a confusion of power)
- Clutter
- A look of "Oh, this hasn't been cleaned in quite a while."

Chi looks everywhere and at all details.

The one-list method is the most surefire way to see (and not just wonder) what needs to get done in your life. It should be a totally *active* list. You write things down, and then cross them off when you've done them. Draw from your one main list, kept in one place (such as a small six-ring binder), to put items on a daily list. Use a calendar for writing appointments and reminders in the same small binder. As soon as you've *written* something on a list, its psychic "voice" is quite muffled. You are no longer hearing, "Do this! Do that!"

Your home should be giving you a big dose of visual serenity and should support you in practical accessibility. Frequently-used things need to be very easily accessible. Adhere to the rule that if a shelf or drawer is at an accessible height for you, its contents should primarily be things that you use often.

VIBRATIONAL CLEANSING

One of feng shui's greatest gifts to the Western world is its acknowledgement of unseen energetic vibrations. In the feng shui worldview, this acknowledgement is understood as basic common sense. Such vibrations can belong to single objects, or they can be hanging around an entire house. If a house or object had previous owners there's a 50-50 chance that it has picked up some vibes. There is also a 50-50 chance that those vibes are excellent and to your benefit, so there is no need for undue paranoia. There is however the small chance that something that was previously owned has picked up vibrations that are not particularly good for you, a sort of "psychic dirt." Once again, there is no need for alarm. Just use incense or a smudge stick to cleanse the old vibrations. (The sage incense from Juniper Ridge is very high quality—see Sources.) The vibration, or residual energy, of previous occupants can be mild or heavy. Everyone can sense it to some degree (although some people have cultivated the ability more than others). If it is an entire residence that you feel needs cleansing, sometimes called space clearing, here are some tips:

- Do it during the day.
- Have every window open as fully as possible. Let the natural breezes do some of the work for you.
- If the place is physically dirty, do a thorough, detailed cleaning of the entire space in conjunction with the vibration cleansing. Preferably do the physical cleaning first.
- Walk the entire inside perimeter of each room, including closets. Go in a clockwise direction, which means turning to your left as soon as you have entered the room.
- Carry burning incense or a sage smudge stick.
- If you can manage it, carry a pure-sounding bell, and ring it every few steps. If someone is assisting you, one can carry the incense, and the other can carry the bell.
- If no bell is readily available, don't worry, you were born with the right tool—use your hands and clap. Don't clap as if you were applauding. Do single, loud, sharp claps when you get to corners and doorways and any place that feels a little unusual—any kind of unusual. It is an extremely powerful, assertive thing to do. You are using your own hands to claim your rightful ownership of a space. It works oh-so-well! Clap high and clap low. There is no way that you can clap and hold incense at the same time, so if you are doing this alone, you will have to make two complete circuits.
- Sing, chant, or speak aloud—whichever you are most comfortable with. The ancient chant "Om" is always good. Absolutely anything that expresses your intention is appropriate. You could simply say, "Peace to this space," over and over. Your voice should sound assertive and be rather loud. Don't worry about the neighbors. This is most likely to be a one-time occurrence, and even if they can hear you, they'll get over it.
- Make sure the smoke from the incense wafts high and low. Bring the incense near the floor and the ceiling, in every corner, including closets and cabinets. Do an ultra-thorough job. It's okay if it takes a while. You are not going to be doing it every day.

If, after doing all this in your home, you are still concerned because of unexplainable, uncomfortable feelings, it may be time to call in an expert. I'm referring to any psychic with an excellent reputation who knows how to do "ghost-busting." Buddhist priests are also recommended in this regard. You *can* find someone if you set your mind to it.

When buying a house, try to find out something about the history of the previous owners. If the house is being sold due to divorce or bankruptcy, the deal may look good, but look at the property from a feng shui point of view. If you notice something that might indicate hard times, such as a missing Fortunate Blessings area, or a stove and refrigerator right next to each other, you might want to be sure that you can correct the situation. Otherwise, history may repeat itself.

Any part of a building that seems unusually dark is probably harboring stagnant energy. It can be a room, or part of a room, or most of a house. Lighten it with higher-wattage bulbs or lighter paint. Also try to bring fresh air to it. Use a fan if necessary. One of the best solutions is the kind of light where the heat of the bulb causes a moving image to rotate, making moving light throughout the space.

The first and fundamental attitude to have toward any object that you own or any space that will shelter you is gratitude. It is the basis of all true spirituality and is always appropriate (even if it is your intention to eventually move).

USED OBJECTS

Exactly the same principles that apply to space clearing also apply to object clearing. It is the vibrational cleansing of an object. You can pass any object (new or used) through incense or sage smoke, and use the sound of your own voice. Saying something as simple as, "I bless this object and welcome it into my life" has an honest directness that penetrates the universe.

Any object can be restored to its original vibrational purity. If you don't feel confident of your ability, ask for professional help.

Every object comes from the body of this planet. Used objects have a natural ecological advantage. The planet is shared by all kinds of people, and no one is exempt from showing respect for the ecosystem. It concerns us all. Any act of compassion for the planet brings groundedness, and the blessings of the earth, into your life.

NON-FENG SHUI TECHNIQUES

These are disciplines that evolved separately from feng shui, but are very complementary.

Dowsing

Dowsing is the ancient art of walking around holding a stick or rod, which then dips down while going over water. It can be very useful to find out if there are underground streams on your property. Dowsing can also locate areas of geopathic stress that may or may not be related to a stream. Don't think that this applies only to country property. A dowser can pinpoint stream locations, even if you live in a townhouse.

Pendulums

A pendulum is a pointed object suspended from a chain or string. The direction of movement of the object answers yes or no questions. Many people like to use a pendulum to bring accuracy to questionable situations. Sometimes a pendulum is used to double-check a decision.

Aromatherapy

Aromatherapy is a recent name for an ancient art, studied by many cultures. How a room or dwelling smells is very important. Diffusing essential oils is the most often-recommended technique in aromatherapy books; scented candles are another. Incense is also commonly used by those who don't mind the bit of smoke. My favorite technique is to grow plants indoors that have fragrant blossoms. Tovah Martin's book, *The Essence of Paradise*, is the best reference on which plants will succeed where.

Vastu

Vastu (sometimes called Vastu Shastra) has its origins in the ancient Indian Vedic civilization. It is both sacred and practical with many applications for modern dwellings. This system for designing buildings and working with space has some similarities with feng shui, yet it is fascinatingly "its own thing." The five elements of Vastu are Fire, Water, Earth, Air, and Space. Books in English on Vastu are not nearly as abundant as feng shui books.

Chapter 9:

Moving

The first step toward a new home is often to improve the home you have now. "Bloom where you are planted" is a wise adage. Time after time I have seen someone make a dump look just gorgeous. Then, out of the blue, comes along the opportunity to move to someplace much nicer. It is as if the Universe were saying, "Well, you did a great job on that one. Let's see what you can do with *this* one." Give a word of thanks for your old home, regardless of how grateful you may be to be leaving it. It sheltered you.

LOCATING A NEW HOME

If you are buying land on which to build your house, get good landform. The land should rise up behind the house site, but not too steeply. Ideally, there should also be a slight rise on each side of the house site. The land in front of the house site should slope down and away from the house. If there is a natural water feature, it should be in front of the house site, not behind it. A house built in this "armchair position" is powerful because the land protects it without obstructing it.

Absolutely everyone is intuitive to some degree. Even if you don't normally think of yourself as intuitive, when you are deciding which new home to live in, be very aware of how you *feel* about the neighborhood as you approach a potential new home for the first time (and any time thereafter). When I say "new home," I'm referring to *new for you*. Building a new house, or buying a brand new house, are not feng shui prerequisites for a fabulous life. It does not matter whether you buy or live in a new home or a used one. Any confused or unsettled bits of past karma may need cleansing. This is true in a brand-new home as well as in a used one, because construction always disturbs the environment. Many period homes (pre-2000 A.D.) have excellent feng shui energy. Because of burgeoning population, new suburban construction is occasionally built over poorly marked private cemeteries. There are no federal laws in the United States that protect abandoned cemeteries on private property. Local statutes are often inadequate and sometimes unenforced. To all new homeowners, my first advice is to do a space clearing.

These are major deciding factors when deciding which home to buy, or live in:

- Do not buy a house with a totally enclosed bathroom unless you are willing to have it removed before you move in. Period.
- Steps going up to the front door of your new home must have risers. If risers can be installed, there is no problem—just do it ASAP.
- When you step inside the front door, make sure there is no missing area in the far left corner of the residence. That's your "Wealth Corner." If there *is* a missing area there, and you still feel that it is your best choice, go ahead. You must, however, be willing to bring back that missing area to the best of your ability. (Suggestions are in Chapter 5.) If this is not done quickly, the new home risks being thought of as a money pit.
- Consider how the element of the house relates to the element of the landscape. The elements of the house and landscape are based upon their shape—primarily their profiles as you approach them. The explanations in Angel Thompson's book *Feng Shui* are quite understandable.

CHECKLIST FOR MOVING

Photocopy this list for use while walking through a potential new home. It is in order by priority of issue.

The best answers are the dotted squares. Checking the dotted squares means "No problem." If you mark an item in a solid square, read the information on the indicated page. If any of the first seven answers is "Yes," I recommend that you don't buy or live in that house.

Yes	No	Item
☐	⬚	Is there a center bathroom? Pages 58, 59, & 60.
☐	⬚	Does the landscape slope steeply down behind the house? Pages 1 & 10.
☐	⬚	Is the house exposed on a hilltop or along the edge of the ocean? Pages 9 & 10.
☐	⬚	Do you suspect high electromagnetic fields? If so, measure them. Pages 97 & 98.
☐	⬚	Is the lot triangular? Pages 89 & 90.
☐	⬚	Are there interior upward stairs in a direct line with the front door, visible from just inside the front door? Page 15.
☐	⬚	Is there a central spiral staircase? Page 15.
⬚	☐	Are there risers on the front stairs? Page 5.

Yes	No	Item
☐	☐	Does the land gently slope down in front of the house, and gently slope up behind the house? Page 10.
☐	☐	Is either of the two back corners of the home "missing"? Page 64.
☐	☐	Is there a tree directly in front of the front door? Pages 1 & 2.
☐	☐	Is the back yard at least as big as the front yard? Page 91.
☐	☐	Is a T-intersection aimed at the house? Page 3.
☐	☐	Are there open beams? Page 24.
☐	☐	Is the house next to a very busy highway? Page 9.
☐	☐	If the road curves, is the house on the concave (inward) side of the curve? Pages 2 & 3.
☐	☐	Are there poison arrows from neighborhood features? Pages 8 & 9.
☐	☐	Is the outline of the floor plan a perfect square or rectangle? Page 62.

Yes	No	Item
☐	☐	Is the outline of the lot a perfect square or rectangle? Pages 89 & 90.
☐	☐	Is it a split-level house? Page 74.
☐	☐	Is the lot a trapezoid with the back property line longer than the front property line? Page 90.
☐	☐	Is there a door between the main bedroom and its bathroom? Page 77.
☐	☐	Are there entire walls of floor-to-ceiling windows? Page 14.
☐	☐	Is a skylight over the stove, bed, or desk area? Page 74.
☐	☐	Are there windows or a back door directly in line with the front door? Pages 13 & 14.
☐	☐	In the kitchen, are water appliances (sink and fridge) adequately separated from fire appliances (oven and range top)? Page 74.
☐	☐	Do any rooms have a central support pole? Page 72.
☐	☐	Can the doorknob of any door touch the doorknob of any other door? Page 68.

Yes	No	Item
☐	☐	Does the main bedroom have an empowered position for the bed? Pages 19 & 20.
☐	☐	Is the house directly next door to a cemetery, mortuary, police station, fire station, or church? Pages 8 & 9.
☐	☐	Is there a center staircase or fireplace? Pages 57 & 73.
☐	☐	Is a pool directly behind the center of the house? Page 113.
☐	☐	Do any important rooms have ceilings that seem too high or too low? Page 78.

Chapter 10:

Gardening

Gardening is a basic and marvelous skill to acquire. Whether you garden indoors or out, it is a rewarding and fulfilling art to study. Plants (both living and artificial) can mute the effects of poison arrows within your home and in the landscape outside. Trees and hedges can be protective and act as guardians. The most effective guardian trees are tall and old, and are best located behind your house.

LANDSCAPING

Some aspects of landscaping, primarily those dealing with the front yard, are discussed in the first chapter. The best yards have lush, healthy landscaping. The worst yards are totally paved. A paved yard stifles the energy from the earth and makes a place look barren. The best solution for a totally paved yard is to remove some of the concrete. If that cannot be done, stain it an earth tone and do container gardening. If there is already grass, but not much else, start planting. Plants with rounded leaves are preferred.

Pathways in general should vary in width in order to take advantage of their ability to "funnel" chi into a dwelling. They should therefore be somewhat wider when they are at their farthest distance from the house. This can often be gracefully accomplished by flaring the pathway where it meets a public sidewalk, or any other destination away from your house. As a general rule, make all paths meander somewhat. Avoid long, straight, paths, especially if the *edges* are straight lines. If you have such paths (such as long straight cement walkways) allow the plants on each side to grow over the walkway a bit. Don't do severe edge trimming, as this only emphasizes the straightness.

If any of the statuary in your garden is spiritually significant, raise it off the ground in whatever way is appropriate and safe for the statue.

Evergreens are an important symbol in feng shui. They come in all sizes; so don't just think of them as big trees. If you live in a climate where plants drop their leaves in winter, evergreens can counter that "dead" look. Evergreen hedges are especially important because they maintain your privacy and establish your borders.

Establishing privacy is considered by many to be a number-one goal in gardening. If this is feasible in your situation, go for it. It will probably mean that you will feel freer to visit areas of your yard or property where you might otherwise seldom go (especially if they are quite in public view). Try to spend time in, and pay attention to the feel of, each area in your yard. Establishing privacy in your yard also creates an area of tranquility where peaceful energy can build up and influence the home positively.

PRUNING

Pruning hedges is a straightforward chop-chop for many people, and that is definitely okay unless the hedge seems quite long. A long, straight, box-trimmed hedge is never expressive of a plant's true form and can definitely cause chi energy to speed up too much. If that seems to be the case, find some way to soften the line. Your goal (according to feng shui) is to allow your plants to "scoop up and funnel in" the chi energy that is going past your lot. Often, straight boxy hedges just escort chi energy past your property at a brisk pace. If planting a new hedge, consider:

- A relatively untrimmed hedge of mixed plantings. (Any good local nursery will have suggestions appropriate to your climate.)
- A serpentine formal hedge. Not only does it most definitely slow chi energy down, it says "Wow!" if done nicely. (Note—*any time* you've made something on your property that says, "Wow!" you have done a primo job of pulling in chi energy.)

Other than for formal hedges, all pruning should be done considering the natural growth form of the particular plant.

Pruning is an essential part of horticulture. You do it every time you remove leaves that are dying on a houseplant. If you don't know how to prune like an expert, please learn. *Never leave a stub!* Those stubs are not allowing the plant to heal over the wound effectively and quickly. Until the wood is sealed, the plant is more susceptible to bugs and disease. The stubs are also potential poison arrows (depending on their size).

Make sure no trees or shrubs are *hugging* your house. It has a stifling effect on your life.

THE FIVE ELEMENTS

It is important to bring as many of the five elements as possible into your landscape. Try to do so in the appropriate area of the bagua.

Earth

Use stones or bricks on walls or pathways. Large boulders are excellent focal points, and were frequently used in ancient Chinese gardens to symbolize mountains. Planters and garden ornaments made of clay are another way to bring in this element.

Wood

Every plant in your garden symbolizes wood—even grass. Trees are, of course, ideal, because the wood is real, and not just symbolized. Wood lawn furniture and bamboo windchimes also express this element.

Fire

Exterior lighting is often the simplest way to bring in this element. If installing exterior lighting seems intimidating to you, consider using tiny clear holiday lights— "fairy lights." Also, outdoor cooking areas are an appropriate way to bring fire into your yard. Attracting wildlife (through bird feeders, et cetera) is also a way to bring the "fire of life" into your landscape.

Metal

Metal garden ornaments and lawn furniture are the easiest way to bring metal into the landscape. You don't have to use both. Some people simply don't like metal chairs, and that is certainly understandable. Reflective metal balls are back in vogue for gardens. The blue-colored ones are great for the Fortunate Blessings area. Outdoor metal windchimes should be used with great consideration for any neighbors who might hear them. Don't be shy about asking your neighbors if the sound is pleasant or disturbing to them. It is best to know! If you are disturbing your neighbors (even if you're not aware of it) you are attracting negative energy. If that is a possible consideration in your area, use bamboo windchimes or very small metal windchimes, so that the sound is more gentle. Metal swingsets or play equipment are a good option for people with young children.

Water

Fountains, pools, and birdbaths are all fairly common ways to introduce the water element. Swimming pools also work, but a large, prominent, swimming pool directly behind a house can signify an abyss. It is often recommended that it be visually screened from the house. Upward-shaped plants in clay pots would be perfect fix. For good measure, you could also put a small mirror outside the house facing the pool. The mirror is symbolically pushing away the influence of the pool.

A kidney-shaped pool should always have the *concave* part facing the house. The Fortunate Blessings area is always ideal for water fountains and birdbaths. Flowing water symbolizes blessings flowing into your life, and a pool represents a reserve of good fortune.

THE BAGUA OUTSIDE

The bagua is laid down over an entire plot of land, encompassing the front and back yards. If, however, the back yard is a separate space, fenced off from the front yard, it can be considered to have a full bagua all of its own. The Fortunate Blessings area is located in the back left corner. Don't have a compost heap there, or in the Fame area. Any other area is fine; since most folks want the compost somewhat removed from the house, there is absolutely nothing wrong with a compost heap in the Relationship area. A heck of a lot of microbial relating has to happen to create rich, healthy humus. The Relationship area is also a great place for a food garden or a clothesline. It is the perfect area for lawn furniture. Whenever lawn furniture is placed on your property, give some thought to its color in relation to that area of the bagua on your land.

As you lay the bagua over your property, note the colors that are appropriate for each area. Plants that bring in those colors are a great way to use feng shui in the landscape. Flower color is not the only way. Variegated leaf color is often more long- lasting and maintenance-free. Dark purple leaf color is excellent in three areas: Knowledge, Life's Path, and Helpful People.

The Fortunate Blessings area of your yard should be stunning. If it is used as an unattended catchall area for storing "junk," you've got some work to do! This opportunity should be viewed positively, since you actually have a great chance to "reintroduce yourself" to the Universe, and bring in some wonderful fortunate blessings, perhaps in the form of money. If there is an outbuilding in that part of your property, it should look good on the outside, and be orderly inside.

If there's just no way to make the Relationship area outside look pink and inviting and romantic, then at least put two coins face-to-face in that corner. They can be buried in the ground, and they don't need to be valuable coins. They should be of the appropriate genders for the relationship you have or the relationship you want. United States coins with images of real women on them can be hard to find, but the Alabama quarter has Helen Keller. Though she was blind and deaf, she saw and knew more than most people.

HOUSEPLANTS

Plants are conscious life. They can enchant an interior like nothing else. Think of your home as an *interior landscape.*

Do not have too many *drooping* houseplants—plants that hang down below their pot. This can add depression to your household. Also do not allow plants to touch the ceiling. This says that you have reached your limit in the gua where the plant is located.

It is important that a houseplant be healthy. If plant is having a hard time, and you are nursing it along, make sure that it is not in the Fortunate Blessings area.

A word about bonsai—*true bonsai* keeps a plant in the same pot for possibly hundreds of years, using wires to dwarf it. Such techniques are frowned upon in feng shui, because of the stunted chi energy. Plants that are naturally small or dwarfed can be charming and do not create a feng shui problem. Such plants can be used to make a miniature landscape, which can include a fountain. Another type of miniature landscape that most definitely has the feng shui seal of approval is "nature aquariums." These have been popularized by author Takashi Amano, and they look like a tiny, very natural underwater landscapes. The fish are always small and often in schools, and plants and stones are the main elements. The serenity and visual harmony of these aquariums is almost hard to believe.

THORNY PLANTS

Whether the plants are grown on the exterior or interior of your home, thorns are not a good idea. Certain plants evolve thorns as a way of saying to other living things, "stay away." Just like porcupine quills, they are a natural defense. To anyone who has had painful experience with thorns, they are a symbol as understandable as a red-hot stove. The message is for you to avoid (or be extremely cautious of) some part of your space.

When you are emphasizing a particular area of the bagua, you should realize that situations will change as time goes by. You may want to emphasize other bagua areas in a few years. All types of astrology and numerology, Asian and Western, recognize that every person's life is going to go through a unique set of cycles based on their birth time. Even though you may not feel the need to emphasize a particular area right now, you should not deliberately install a message of "don't go there." No areas of the bagua are truly expendable. Missing areas are to be brought back, if only symbolically. Any area that is excessively thorny (such as a cactus collection) is causing you problems. The smaller the place you live in (such as a studio apartment), the more strongly this effect applies. A large plot of several acres has much more leeway because the physical size of a gua can concentrate or dilute an effect.

Plants with spiky leaves that can hurt you, such as yucca and agave (or Century Plant), are to be thought of as thorny plants. The Fame area is the one place where it's OK to have spiky plants like agave or yucca. They do have a strong uprising quality, but they also say, "don't come too close." If you have an ultra-steep downward slope behind your house, which cannot be traversed anyway, agave or yucca could be planted in the Fame area there to raise the energy. Do not ever plant thorny or spiky plants in the Relationship or Fortunate Blessings areas. You can make a Relationship area quite red and pink without the use of roses. I also do not recommend thorny or spiky plants near the entrance to your property, or near a pathway.

Not all spiky plants can hurt you and not every plant with a spiky leaf form is forbidden. Most palm leaves are friendly and durable. Palms with floor uplights behind them enchant the ceiling of a room. If your ceiling is otherwise very plain in the dark hours, that splash of light and natural form can enhance the yang of the space. One particularly easy palm to grow is Rhapis excelsa, the elegant Lady Palm. Palm experts refer to it as "the perfect indoor palm."

Sansevieria (Snake Plant) has sword-shaped leaves, but they won't cut you. They require almost no light, but if given adequate sunlight they will bear very fragrant white flowers. I would not place them indiscriminately in just any gua. They are mainly for uplifting energy around drains, and enhancing the Fame area.

Chapter 11:

Retail Stores

The blunt truth about success in retail is this: You want a particular kind of chi energy (people) to:

- Come into your store
- Give you money
- Leave smiling.

There is an old business adage "the customer pays your salary." Your salary is a form of chi energy, and it ultimately comes from the customer. You have exchanged the energy of your time for a paycheck. Remember what customers are—bundles of chi energy with money (another form of chi energy) in their pockets. This proper understanding of people as chi energy is the *most important* element for continued retail success.

A good landform would be a nice plus, as would no poison arrows, but they are less important in retail. Retail is one of the most yang activities. Its yang nature overrides problems that would be troublesome for a home. The main thing is a good location and good signage. The easier you make it for people to give you money, the more money they will give you. Money is the form of energy that fuels your store. Invite it graciously, and welcome it smiling.

THE FRONT

Location, location, location. They're the first three commonsense rules about retail. People need to easily see your store, or at least your signage. If they can't find you, you won't prosper. Get your potential customer's attention—boldly and attractively. (That word "attractive" is important. If you don't *attract* people, you sure won't get their money.) A good sign is often the first way to improve retail business. Kat Wilson of Back to the Drawing Board, a sign company in San Francisco, says, "You only have a few seconds to get people's attention when they're on the street."

You get what you ask for with signage in retail. Very readable fat letters are a must. Fat letters say abundant and successful. Use fat, bountiful, letters on door and street signs or any time the name of your business is presented to the public, such as on business cards and stationery.

If your business is located in a part of town that is multilingual, make sure some of your staff is multilingual, and then *add it to your signage* and watch your business grow.

Carefully done, *neon is close to ultimate* for attracting chi energy during the dark hours. As far as the daylight hours are concerned, do not forget your number-one goal—*get their attention*—and do it well. One of the most important things is to use red on the outside. A red doormat is appropriate for many stores. If you are fortunate enough to have planters outside your door, use red planters or grow red plants—leaf or flower color. Make maximum use of space in public view. In display windows and along the sidewalk, use:

- Light
- Motion
- The color red.

If you use the color green on an exterior sign, restrict it to one-fourth or less of the total size. Too much green will camouflage the sign.

Physical Layout

One of the most important things *not to do* is to aim poison arrows at your customers as soon as they walk in the door, with the right-angle edges of island display units and sales/wrap counters. I used to pass by a small, charming, new-and-used bookstore that was doing just about everything wrong, feng shui-wise. I was quite fond of the store, and one day I offered the owner a bit of advice about the worst of his problems. The first island shelving unit was aiming a fierce poison arrow directly at the door. I had never seen a single customer in the store in all the times I had passed by it. I suggested that the owner move a spinning card rack in front of the offending corner. The next time I walked by the store, I saw that he had done so. I also saw that his small store had so many customers that I could not comfortably squeeze in the door. I walked on by, but with a big smile on my face.

Empower cashiers and any reception personnel by giving them a clear view of the door—without being in a direct line with the entrance. It is usually best not to have stairs in a direct line with the entrance door. If the stairs are not too close to the door, there is no problem.

Large stores often need support poles to hold up the roof. It is best to disguise them as much as possible. They can be incorporated into merchandise display.

The bagua in a retail store is exactly 100% the same as the bagua in a residence, although quite a bit less powerful because no one actually lives in the store. The same principles for each bagua area apply. See Chapter 4. In particular, these five guas (in order of importance) should be enhanced:

- Fortunate Blessings
- Fame
- Relationship
- Helpful People
- Life's Path

The Fortunate Blessings gua is (as usual) of crucial importance. This area is a prime candidate for displaying your most expensive merchandise. Quite often, it is possible to enhance a gua by putting the correct color merchandise there. Do make sure that there is fairly direct access from the door to the Fortunate Blessings area. I have occasionally recommended that the entire back wall of a store be painted red (any shade). This can be helpful for bringing chi fully into a store and circulating it well. If you have ever considered having a fountain in your store, two of the best areas are near the cash register(s) and/ or near the door. If your store has a sound system, I would not recommend playing the radio. The boosted volume of commercials is jarring to chi, and rarely encourages customers to linger.

BUSINESS HOURS

Your store is like a fountain—it only works when it is on. A well-lighted *open* store attracts chi energy (including people).

Shopping at a store is a somewhat yang activity—compared to shopping on the Internet (your new competition). Internet sales can take place twenty-four hours a day. The least a store can do is to have an answering machine with its hours, preferably allowing the customer to leave a message. The time when your physical retail store is open to the public is vital time—the more the better. Working people work nine to five; after that, they are much more available to spend the money they've just earned. If you are not open evenings and weekends you are missing the boat. It's your best opportunity to "harvest" money because these are the optimum shopping hours for many people. It *is* time-specific. Stores that have expanded their days and hours are often surprised by the effusion of gratitude coming from customers. That tells you everything.

WEBSITES

Websites are utterly different from retail stores. They are virtual spaces, not physical spaces so the same rules just don't apply. Get a good web designer and keep it pretty simple—the fewer ads and distractions the better. I read about a company in California that (on the advice of a feng shui consultant) made the background of their website red and the lettering a darker red. They said, "People tell us it's hard to read, but we know it's good feng shui." I rolled my eyes and thought of P. T. Barnum: "There's a sucker born every minute."

Chapter 12:

Offices

Many people are wary about where they work. They may have a niggling feeling that *something* is wrong, but they can't quite put their finger on it—and even if they could, they might not feel empowered to do anything about it. Many owners and bosses discourage office changes or personalizing workspaces. They are shortsighted. A truly intelligent manager will allow (and encourage) workers to personalize their desks, as long as it isn't wildly out of place. The most important thing about your desk is that you be able to see the main door. If you cannot, use a mirror. If you have business cards, the Fame area of your desk is a very good place for them. As you are sitting at your desk, that area is in the far middle. A red business card holder would be an appropriate feng shui enhancement. (Other tips for desks are in the sections on Empowered Positions and Home Offices.)

Because of computers and electronic technology, desks are often somewhat L-shaped. Where you spend most of your time at the desk determines the orientation of the bagua—in most cases. Please be aware of the strong poison arrows that are often caused by these desk shapes, and try not to sit in the path of one. Also try not to have the sharp right angle of a filing cabinet aimed at you.

Your desk chair should be comfortable, and preferably have a solid back. Like a solid headboard, a desk chair that covers your back completely (without gaps) is considered ideal. It conveys the vibration of "solid backing" to your decisions. It can also serve to protect you from poison arrows coming from behind.

Throughout the room or rooms of the office, apply the bagua map. Avoid having an open trashcan in the Fortunate Blessings area. Instead, something striking like a large, healthy, plant would be great.

WAITING ROOMS

Many professional offices have waiting rooms. The most important factors include:

Poison arrows

Do not let the shape of the reception desk cast a poison arrow at the entrance. Do not allow filing cabinets or other furniture to cast poison arrows at the reception personnel. Presumably no one client is going to be sitting in the waiting room for hours on end, day after day. Poison arrows (pointing at clients) are never a good idea, but you can certainly make do with them if you must. I would, however, refrain from using glass-top tables, unless the glass is rimmed.

Appropriate empowerment

Empower the reception personnel by allowing a clear view of the entrance door. The reception desk should not be in a direct line with that particular door. If there is no choice but to have a reception desk in a direct line with the entrance, then put a plant on the desk. Tuck a tiny mirror inside the pot, with the shiny side facing the door. Try to place it in a direct line between the door and the reception personnel. You could use a faceted clear crystal object, such as a paperweight, instead of a plant. Always enhance these three areas: Fortunate Blessings, Fame, and Relationship. You won't be sorry! Depending on the type of office, also enhance the Health or Knowledge areas.

Recommended Reading

As people begin to read about feng shui, first they are intrigued. Then, as they read more, they get confused. The confusion inevitably comes from the fact that one of feng shui's most powerful tools, a grid called the bagua, is used very differently by two different schools of feng shui, compass-oriented and entrance-oriented (also called Form or Landform School). The problem is further compounded by the fact that almost never does a single book mention that there is another way to do it. It's not much of a problem when feng shui schools disagree about fairly minor things, like mirrors in a bedroom (Steven Post says the more the merrier). But placement of the bagua is central to the practice of feng shui. Most other aspects of feng shui are either universal or their differences are differences of emphasis. Any time a feng shui book disagrees with the information in another book, ask yourself which author is giving you reasons. If the author isn't taking the time to explain the rationale, I have to wonder if they themselves even know the reason why.

If a book asks when you were born, and mentions that certain numbers or directions are good for you, but others aren't, that's a Compass School book. If a book never mentions those two things, it's most likely a Form School book, and there are many sub-schools under the vast and ancient umbrella of Form School. The Form School books will rarely, if ever, refer to anything as "lucky." Form School's advice is based on the form of things (what they are shaped like) and how that form affects the flow of energy.

Also listed are books on topics that are related to feng shui. For more book reviews, please consult my Web site, fungshway.com, which is devoted to reviewing feng shui literature.

There are close to a thousand feng shui books in English. So how do you separate the wheat from the chaff? Know your authors—that's how! Certain authors seem to be incapable of writing a bad or trivial book. (Trivial books have indeed flooded the market with one prolific author being responsible for most of them. She will remain unnamed, but you can probably guess).

So here's the *crème de la crème* (in my opinion) of feng shui authors—in alphabetical order.

Simon Brown—Brown is perhaps the least confusing of the Compass School writers. His colorful books are quite inviting and good for anyone of any school.

Karen Rauch Carter—Carter's use of humor is unique and heartwarming. She's never condescending and truly knows how to write a page-turner. I eagerly await a sequel to *Move Your Stuff, Change Your Life*. Many people have told me it was *the* book that meant the most to them. That's saying a lot!

Terah Kathryn Collins—Her books have been extremely important in my life and I've recommended them for many years. She emphasizes the use of affirmations when making feng shui adjustments, and I couldn't agree more. (In my opinion, your angels could think you are just doing strange decorating unless you *say* the reason why.)

Richard Craze—Compass feng shui has two prolific Richards—Richard Craze and Richard Webster. Steer clear of Richard Webster (his feng shui books are garbled) and set your compass by Richard Craze. Craze's explanation of the bagua is truly through.

Clear Englebert—Since *Feng Shui Demystified* was first published in 2000, I've had two more feng shui books published: *Bedroom Feng Shui* and *Feng Shui for Hawaii*. The bedroom is the most important room in the home and for many people it is the only room that they can control. My book covers every aspect of the bedroom and its relation to feng shui. It is also available in German.

Feng Shui for Hawaii is not just for Hawaii—it's for any home anywhere. Most of the pictures were taken in Hawaii, and for that reason it's one of the most beautiful feng shui books ever published. It's also one of the most understandable. The color photos on every page pull you along through the book and leave no doubt what's being explained. Both books amplify topics discussed in *Feng Shui Demystified* and also cover other areas.

Carole Hyder—Hyder's books don't just touch your heart, they reach deep within and touch your soul. Her *Living Feng Shui* is without a doubt the most readable feng shui book ever written.

Daniel David Kennedy—He's a very careful and complete writer, and even though I find the "for Dummies" series condescending and irritating (with ugly covers), his book in that series is a miracle of completeness.

Karen Kingston—Her *Clear Your Clutter with Feng Shui* will turn you into a feng shui zombie (in a good way!) and you *will* follow her advice and live a clutter-free life. There's *power* in them there words!

Gina Lazenby—Lazenby does not waste words, and she does not waste pictures. Both are used to great advantage in her wonderful books. I recommend *The Feng Shui House Book* wholeheartedly—it is glorious. The pictures are accompanied by extensive commentary. She does what almost no other author does—she comments on *everything* in the picture and goes the extra mile by pointing out what else could be done to improve it. She can say in one sentence what other authors require a paragraph for.

Susan Levitt—Levitt writes well on many subjects, and her feng shui books are each unique. She's not the only writer on feng shui for younger folks, but her *Teen Feng Shui* by far the most useful. In *Taoist Feng Shui* she explains how its Taoist roots are intertwined with the *I Ching* and Chinese astrology. Levitt's chapter on astrology called "Reckoning of Fate" is the best of its kind in any book I've seen.

Henry Lin—His book, *The Art and Science of Feng Shui*, is unique and quite eye-opening. He refers to the Form School as the Situation School, which is food for thought. Lin has done his homework, reading and quoting from the original sources in Chinese. From an old Form School classic he quotes, "all depends on [an] individual's intuition." Later in the book he says, "…feng shui is not a set of fixed rules. Instead, it is a body of principles, which willingly lend[s] itself to creative interpretation and application by its students." His history of feng shui is extremely well done, including an extensive background on Yang Yun-song, who was also known as "Savior of the Poor," and is my personal hero. Yang's story is also told in Larry Sang's *The Principles of Feng Shui*.

Evelyn Lip—Lip is an architect as well as a feng shui expert. The subjects of her books are quite varied, but the quality is always top-notch. One of her books even explains how to design business cards and retail store signage.

Sarah Rossbach—She is the reason I practice feng shui! I had only read Compass School books until I read Rossbach and they just didn't appeal to me (too many numbers and things that didn't make common sense). Rossbach was a groundbreaker, and she continues to write books worthy of worship (well, almost).

Nancy SantoPietro— Her books are brilliant achievements, dealing primarily with the interiors. They have some of the most lucid prose and drawings to be found in any feng shui books. They contain information on aromatherapy, crystal and gemstone properties, the chakras, as well as advice on how to get pregnant. SantoPietro's books have become instant classics.

Angel Thompson—The basic chi that first comes into our lives does so under the influence of the larger environment. Do not underestimate its importance!
Thompson's *Feng Shui* has the clearest information on the external environment. There's an especially good section on how the landscape of your house (or lot) interacts with the larger landscape of your area. Many books have tried to present this very complicated information in an understandable way. Thompson succeeds.

Nancilee Wydra—Wydra is prolific and for good reason—she has a lot to say and she knows how to say it. Her *Feng Shui: Principles for Building and Remodeling* (co-authored with architect Lenore Baigelman) however has examples of interior bathrooms, which I think are a horrible idea.

Eva Wong—I learned that a feng shui consultant shouldn't be referred to a "master" until they are at least 81 years old (experience matters). Eva Wong is the one exception I'd make to that rule. She knows Compass and Landform Schools backward and forward and through to the marrow.

Baolin Wu—His *Lighting the Eye of the Dragon* will have you hooked by the end of the first paragraph—no joke! I pray he will write more feng shui books. Nobody else says what he says, and we all need to learn more of what he has to teach.

Related Topics

The Book of Changes and the Unchanging Truth by Hua Ching Ni

The I Ching is considered by many to be the oldest written book in the world. It is a Taoist oracle—a wise friend offering advice in troublesome situations. It is not advisable to overuse it. It offers a *larger* view, often giving very specific and lucid advice in situations that really have you stumped.

Whether or not one connects well with this fine book largely depends upon the translation that you use. There are now many *I Ching* translations. The Wilhelm/Baynes translation from Princeton University Press is the old standard, but I feel that *The Book of Changes and the Unchanging Truth* is now the finest translation available. Master Ni is from an ancient lineage of Taoist masters. He knows with his bones what he is translating. I unreservedly recommend this translation.

Getting Organized by Stephanie Winston (audio)

Organizing is basic to feng shui, but sayin' it and doin' it are two very different things! For some people, to be organized is a major lifestyle challenge. The outcome can seem attractive, but getting from here to there can be daunting. The good news is that this audio of *Getting Organized* can seep into you by osmosis. Keep listening to it until you are doing it—all of it. Stephanie Winston does cover all of it—every aspect of being organized. Her voice carries a confidence that helps get you there. I've read scores of organizing books, and this one stands high—especially the audio version.

Speed Cleaning by Jeff Campbell

Cleaning is as essential to feng shui as breathing is to life. This is by far the best book on cleaning ever published. It should be taught in schools, because sooner or later everybody's gotta do some cleaning—may as well be smart about it. As in feng shui, this book isn't afraid to state the obvious. Some rules are shockingly simple, as in, "work from top to bottom," "if it isn't dirty, don't clean it," "pay attention," but when applied together, they make for fast, efficient cleaning.

Spring Cleaning by Jeff Campbell

Jeff Campbell's *Speed Cleaning* covers the weekly or biweekly basics and this subsequent book covers just about all the rest. Almost everybody has windows, and way too many are dirty most of the time. It is empowering to have the knowledge and skill to clean one's windows quickly and efficiently. He gives step-by-step instructions for every conceivable kind of window. No paper towels, no newspapers, no blue chemical spray, and no streaks! A good squeegee is your friend.

Campbell gives you the do's and don't of polishing metal, how to clean carpets, walls, and floors, and much more. I rarely have need to do some of the things this book covers (such as stripping off a floor finish) but should the need arise, I know I can count on Jeff Campbell to have done *all* the research for me. Even though he explains in detail how to wash a ceiling, his first advice is don't (unless you absolutely have to). He is reasonable, readable, and wonderful. I recommend this book unreservedly. Every homeowner and probably every renter should have a copy of this fine book.

Vimala Rodgers

Rodgers has written two amazing books on handwriting which explain the energetics of how we form the letters we write. I think of this as the feng shui of handwriting—after all we are creating a physical form as we write. The details of our life do matter. Her books are: *Change Your Handwriting, Change Your Life* and more recently, *Your Handwriting Can Change Your Life*.

Glossary

Bagua mirror

A mirror with an octagonal (eight-sided) frame, with the *I Ching* trigrams around the eight sides. If it doesn't have the trigrams, it's just an octagon mirror and not a bagua mirror. A mirror with the Chinese animals around it is also not a bagua mirror. For more information about the trigram arrangement in the bagua, read the yin/yang chapter in *Feng Shui: A Complete Guide* by Richard Craze. It's an extraordinarily lucid explanation.

The bagua mirror may have a blue-tinted plastic film sticking to the glass when you buy it. The film was to protect the glass before purchase. Remove that film before using the mirror. Otherwise, it won't be very effective.

Don't use a bagua mirror unless you need it. It shouldn't be used indiscriminately to "bring in good energy." It is a mirror; it reflects away. Bagua mirrors are available through the Internet, or at Chinese knick-knack stores. They represent good order, and are considered powerful. Almost *never* use them inside. They are primarily for outside use. Also be very sure to hang them correctly, with the three solid yang lines at the top. In that orientation they symbolize a "house of the living." If the mirror were turned upside down, it would be for a "house of the dead"—a mausoleum.

Casement Window

To open these windows, a crank handle is turned, and the windows open out on hinges along the vertical edge. If there is a screen, it is on the inside of the glass. Frank Lloyd Wright said that if these windows had not already been invented, he would have invented them. They are treasured for their ability to "catch a breeze" and funnel it into a room. Feng shui loves them because they can (usually) open fully.

Chi (or Qi)

Pronounced *chee* (or *ki* in Japanese). The basic energy of the Universe. Think of it as any form of energy.

Concave

This mirror curves inward—"caves in." It enlarges a very close image, but inverts a distant image. Turning the distant object upside down makes it less important. Use it outside when an overscale object (cliff or skyscraper) dwarfs your building. Concave mirrors absorb harmful energy. See Fig. 33.

Concave mirror

side view

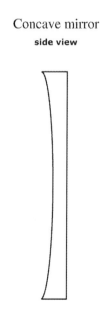

Fig. 33

Convex

This mirror curves outward. It reflects and disperses energy from many directions. They're available where auto supplies are sold. See Fig. 34.

Convex mirror

side view

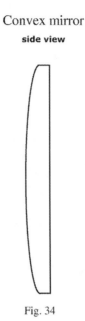

Fig. 34

Directionology

This amazing aspect of Taoist astrology and numerology can tell you which directions are best (and worst) for you to move towards. The calculations are based upon when you were born. Each year, the auspicious directions will change. You are considered to be in the center of the compass.

Double-Hung Window

These windows were popular in your great-grandparents' time and they are still much used today. The bottom half slides up and (one hopes) the top slides down. They are not a feng shui favorite because the window opening is always at least half blocked by the glass. In my experience, many double-hung windows become painted shut over time. Unstick 'em, for God's sake! Actually, you'll be doing it for your own sake. They were meant to function fully and they've been made dysfunctional by some layers of paint. Hardware and paint stores sell a special tool for doing the job. It is shaped like a flat trowel with serrated edges. Be sure to use protection so that you don't breathe (potentially lead-contaminated) paint dust. Once both halves of the window can open well, you'll have restored better air circulation to the building and eliminated some dysfunction from your life. Even so, double-hung windows are never as ideal as windows that can open fully.

Elements

There are five elements according to Taoism. The word Element here has absolutely nothing to do with the Periodic Table of Elements of Western science. In Taoism they refer to archetypal energies. See the Chart of Bagua Areas (in Chapter 3) for easy reference to things that represent the elements. Consult these columns:
Main element
Color
Shape
Comments

Fame area

One of the nine areas in the bagua map. It is concerned with what is being said about you.

Fortunate Blessings area

One of the nine areas in the bagua map. It is typically called the Wealth area and, as such, has become a buzzword for feng shui.

Gua

The Chinese name for any of the nine bagua areas. Guas is the plural.

Magnetic sleep pad

A pad with magnets in it, which usually goes under your mattress, providing an even, negative, magnetic field for your body. There are several reputable manufacturers. See Sources for one of them.

Mirror, Small Flat

These are the mirrors that I use the most. They are available at craft supply stores. Some are quite tiny and can be used discreetly. Any flat mirror reflects energy directly back. See also Concave Mirror, Convex Mirror.

Poison arrow

This harsh or malevolent chi energy has various names: sha chi, or shar. It is chi energy that has encountered something in the environment to cause it to speed up or get irritated.

Risers

Risers are the vertical parts of stairs that connect the treads, which you step on. When you walk upstairs they are the part that your toes are pointing towards.

Trigram

The basic unit of a trigram is a line, either solid or with an opening in it.

A yin line with an   A solid yang line
opening in the center

When combined in units of three lines, there only eight possible combinations. They are listed on the Chart of Bagua Areas (in Chapter 3) with their meanings. Also see Recommended Reading, *The Book of Changes and the Unchanging Truth*—an excellent translation of the *I Ching* and exposition of the trigrams.

Windcatcher

A windcatcher is a decorative item that moves in the wind but is silent. Whirligigs, windsocks, and banners are examples. They attract energy because they move. Avoid the kind that point downward.

Acknowledgments

I offer gratitude to Steve Mann, Rick Mears, Caryle Hirshberg, and Elaine Gill. Their help and encouragement was instrumental in the birthing of this book. I also offer eternal thanks to my wonderful parents Merle Twitty Englebert and Robert William Englebert. They were public school teachers for a combined sixty-two years. My teaching ability is largely inherited from them.

Sources

Alphalab, 800-658-7030, www.trifield.com
They sell gaussmeters for measuring EMFs – electromagnetic fields.

Karizma, 415-861-4515, Karizma1@att.net
Excellent source for tiny wind chimes.

Mirror Mirror, 808-945-4312, peonylane@yahoo.com
Beautiful jade bagua mirrors, and tiny windchimes of fine quality.

Juniper Ridge, 800-205-9499, www.juniperridge.com
A source of excellent sage incense for clearing.

Xinacat Prisms and Crystal Jewelry, http://stores.shop.ebay.com/XinaCat-Prisms-and-Crystal-Jewelry
An eBay store with an excellent selection of crystals at decent prices.

Silver Leaf Wallpaper, www.wallliner.com has a silver leaf wallpaper (CW2600) that can serve to energetically seal a room. In a damp room, other kinds of reflective materials run the risk of mildew or mold behind them. Never let this happen. If in doubt, ask a building professional.

Magnetic sleep pad
MAGNETICo, Calgary, Alberta, Canada 800-265-1119, magneticosleep. com.

Index

Affirmation   2, 39, 123

Altar   56, 82, 83

Ancestors   38. See Health and Family Area

Animals 10, 52, 88

Animals, the Four   10

Apartment   1, 6, 43, 45, 54, 57, 58, 59, 79, 95, 115

Aquarium   51, 55, 114

Aromatherapy   103

Bagua Mirror   128

Bamboo flutes   24

Bathroom   13, 14, 15, 39, 41, 46, 52, 54, 58, 59, 60, 61, 75, 76, 77, 84, 88, 92, 94, 99, 105, 125

Bathtub 24, 88

Beams   xi, 24, 25, 107

Bed   19, 20, 23, 24, 26, 44, 57, 78, 80, 81, 82, 94, 97, 98

Birdfeeder   64, 65, 66

Blinds   21, 25, 71

Bonsai   114

Books   iv, 36, 39, 53, 55, 56, 93, 98, 99, 103, 122, 123, 124, 125, 126, 127, 141

Bookshelf   55, 70

Bullnose   27, 50

Bumper stickers 96

Career   38, 55, 56, 76. See Life's Path Area

Cemetery   9, 109

Center Area   57

Centipede   9

Chandelier   74

Chi   6, 7, 9, 10, 12, 13, 14, 15, 19, 20, 24, 26, 28, 29, 32, 47, 51, 69, 71, 73, 74, 79, 81, 83, 96, 97, 100, 111, 114, 116, 118, 129, 132

Chi, attracting / inviting 1, 2, 4, 5, 6, 7, 9, 12, 13, 14, 15, 28, 29, 31, 32, 110, 111, 116, 117, 118, 125

Children and Creativity Area 37, 76, 88

Chiminea   73

Church 8, 9, 88, 109

Coffin   19, 20, 21

Command Position   23

Computer   21, 22, 39, 49, 54, 56, 76, 87, 95, 98, 120

Condominium 6, 89

Creativity   36, 37, 38, 39, 54, 71, 76, 88. See Children and Creativity Area

Crystal, natural 21, 25, 29, 57, 66, 82

Crystal, prismatic   4, 6, 9, 12,

13, 14, 15, 24, 25, 29, 30, 51, 70, 74, 76, 77, 79, 96, 121, 135

Cul-de-sac   3

Curtains   7, 9, 14, 21, 51, 52, 77, 79

Curtains, sheer   7, 51, 79

Desk   21, 22, 23, 24, 25, 76, 78, 108, 120, 121

Dining table   23, 28, 81, 86

Directionology   130

Door   1, 2, 4, 5, 6, 7, 8, 9, 10, 11, 13, 14, 15, 16, 19, 20, 21, 22, 23, 24, 27, 31, 43, 45, 46, 47, 49, 56, 59, 60, 61, 64, 68, 69, 70, 71, 72, 73, 74, 76, 77, 79, 88, 89, 90, 94, 97, 98, 105, 117, 118, 120, 121

Door, front   1, 2, 4, 5, 6, 7, 10, 11, 15, 46, 47, 60, 61, 73, 74, 89, 90, 105,

Door, glass   13

Door, screen   6, 7

Doorharp   31

Dowel   26, 27

Dowsing   103

Dragon 10, 11, 125

Drains 14, 15, 28, 115

Drapes 9, 13, 14, 56, 71. See Curtains

Driveway   1, 4, 65

Echos   79

Electromagnetic Fields—EMF 106, 135

Fame Area   31, 37, 41, 43, 49, 51, 52, 66, 76, 81, 96, 113, 115, 120, 131

Fan   8, 25, 79, 102

Feathers 39, 52, 82

Fireplace   52, 57, 73, 83, 109

Flowers 4, 32, 33, 53, 54, 66, 67, 76, 82, 85, 115

Flutes   xi, 24

Fortunate Blessings Area 15, 28, 45, 47, 48, 49, 50, 51, 59, 77, 84, 92, 96, 102, 112, 113, 114, 118, 120, 131

Fountain, exterior   6, 10, 11, 32, 65, 113

Fountain, interior   12, 31, 32, 39, 51, 52, 55, 56, 57, 73, 93, 114, 118

Fur   39, 52

Garage 4, 46, 48, 55, 65, 77, 99

Gazing ball   4, 23

Glass   xi, 7, 9, 13, 14, 18, 22, 29, 31, 42, 56, 64, 73, 75, 81, 84, 86, 121, 128, 130

Hallway 12, 13, 24, 76

Health 16, 24, 26, 36, 37, 38, 56, 57, 73, 85, 99, 121. See Health and Family Area

Health and Family Area   36, 37, 38, 56, 57, 73, 99

Helpful People and Travel Area 36, 38, 55, 96, 99, 113, 118

Hinges 6, 7, 68, 128

Hooks 93

Hotel   94

I Ching 2, 37, 39, 44, 49, 51, 53, 54, 55, 56, 57, 124, 126, 128, 132

Keller, Helen   114

Knives xi, 2, 25, 53, 75

Knowledge and Self-Cultivation Area   121

Lava lamps   32

Leather 39, 52

Life's Path Area 41, 43, 45, 55, 88

Lighting, exterior   4, 10, 65, 112

Lighting, interior   12, 24, 25, 32, 53, 54

Loft   78

Love   2, 16, 18, 38, 46, 51, 53,

54, 99. See Relationship Area

Mansard roof   79

Masks   85

Mattress   79, 80, 81, 131

Mayan balls   96

Mirror 2, 3, 4, 8, 9, 13, 14, 15, 16, 19, 20, 21, 22, 23, 24, 25, 49, 52, 56, 59, 60, 61, 64, 68, 72, 75, 77, 79, 82, 83, 84, 89, 90, 91, 96, 113, 120, 121, 128, 129, 131

Mirror, bagua   xi, 2, 3, 9, 14, 15, 28, 34, 36, 37, 43, 44, 45, 46, 47, 48, 49, 50, 57, 59, 62, 66, 74, 76, 88, 90, 91, 95, 96, 97, 112, 113, 115, 118, 120, 122, 123, 128, 131, 135

Mirror, concave 9, 85, 129

Mirror, convex   3, 9, 21, 22, 85, 129, 130

Mother-in-law's-tongue   52, 60, 115. See Sansevieria

Nails   93

Paint   4, 7, 24, 25, 26, 42, 46, 50, 52, 78, 79, 91, 102, 118, 130

Paperweight   76, 121

Pendulum   83, 103

Phoenix 10

Plants   32, 40, 90,

Plants, artificial 1, 24, 32, 33, 54, 73

Plants, dried   32, 33, 85

Plants, exterior   1, 2, 3, 4, 6, 7, 66, 89, 90, 110, 111, 112, 113, 114, 115, 117

Plants, interior   9, 15, 19, 24, 27, 32, 39, 49, 52, 54, 57, 59, 60, 72, 73, 74, 76, 80, 82, 86, 103, 114, 121

Plastic   39, 52

Pottery 4, 39, 53, 56, 57, 73, 75

Red   1, 4, 6, 7, 10, 14, 24, 30, 34, 37, 38, 41, 49, 50, 51, 52, 53, 60, 68, 76, 81, 115, 117, 118, 119, 120

Red ribbons   68

Refrigerator   49, 74, 75, 102

Relationship Area   37, 47, 48, 53, 54, 65, 67, 75, 76, 88, 95, 113, 114, 115

Reputation   38. See Fame Area

Rhapis palm   49, 115

Road   1, 2, 4, 9, 47

Rooster 9

Rug   12, 28, 52, 79

Sansevieria   52, 60, 115

Sauna   98

Shelves 18, 21, 25, 57, 81

Sink   74, 108

Skylights   59, 74, 108

Stairs   5, 6, 15, 57, 84, 106, 118, 132

Stairs, spiral   15, 57

Statues xi, 67, 79, 85

Sticks   15, 81, 82, 100, 101, 103, 135

Stove   22, 23, 24, 74, 75, 83, 88, 102, 115

Stripes 53

Swimming pool 65, 113

Telephone   54, 76, 97, 98

Television   18, 23, 39, 49, 52, 54, 56, 78, 94, 98

Thorns 32, 49, 114

Tiger   10

Toilet   14, 18, 19, 58, 59, 60, 61, 75, 84, 88

Torchiere   25, 53

Tortoise 10

Travel   36, 38, 55, 76, 96. See Helpful People and Travel Area

Trees   1, 2, 8, 40, 57, 73, 90, 110, 111, 112

Trompe-l'oeil   91
Vastu   103
Waterfall   55, 86
Wealth 38, 49, 50, 51, 60, 95, 105,
131. See Fortunate Blessings Area
Weathervane   10
Windchime   4, 6, 9, 13, 14, 15,
24, 51, 60, 64, 74, 79, 112, 113,
135
Window   xi, 7, 8, 9, 13, 14,
19, 21, 23, 25, 51, 62, 64, 65, 66,
67, 71, 72, 79, 84, 91, 97, 101,
117, 127, 128, 130, 131
Window box   65, 66, 67
Wine rack   28

About the Author

Clear Englebert is an internationally acclaimed feng shui consultant and teacher. His previous best-selling books are *Bedroom Feng Shui* and *Feng Shui for Hawaii*. His books are available in four languages. He lives in Kona, Hawaii, and maintains the website fungshway.com.